funtastic family nights

19 Family Night Programs

KURT BICKEL

CPH
SAINT LOUIS

Cover illustration by Michael Fleishman.

Scripture quotations taken from the HOLY BIBLE, NEW INTERNATIONAL VERSION®. NIV®. Copyright © 1973, 1978, 1984 by International Bible Society. Used by permission of Zondervan Publishing House. All rights reserved.

Copyright © 1998 Concordia Publishing House
3558 S. Jefferson Avenue, St. Louis, MO 63118-3968
Manufactured in the United States of America

2   3   4   5   6   7   8   9   10   07   06   05   04   03   02   01   00   99

Contents

INTRODUCTION
Teaching the Faith

Faith nurture happens best in the family. Parents are the most effective teachers for biblical/religious truths and values. Healthy family relationships become the setting in which faith can grow by the power of the Holy Spirit. The activities in this book celebrate the gift of family as a work of the Spirit. These family events seek to affirm Baptism as central to the role of parents as they "bring up [their children] in the training and instruction of the Lord." This resource provides practical designs by which congregations can encourage, enhance, and model family spiritual growth through "faith talk."

Focus on the Positive

Funtastic Family Nights promotes health and growth in families by fostering positive, nurturing relationships. Through these active learning experiences, the church provides a way for families simply to be together and talk about their faith. The topics center on issues that promote a positive family climate. Families will experience joy-filled times together and interact with other families in an atmosphere of support and encouragement.

Research

Search Institute, a nonprofit research organization based in Minneapolis, Minn., surveyed 274,000 teenagers and discovered that a major difference between troubled teens and healthy, productive, positive teens was the presence of certain developmental assets.

Search discovered that these assets were both external and internal. External assets have to do with family, church, and community. These include family support, parents as social resources, parent communication, other adult resources, other adult communication, parent involvement in school, positive school climate, parental standards, parental discipline, parental monitoring, time at home, positive peer influence, music, extracurricular activities, community activities, and involvement with a faith community.

They also identified core values that the child develops internally. These internal assets are achievement motivation, educational aspiration, school performance, homework, helping people, global concern, empathy, sexual restraint, assertiveness skills, decision-making skills, planning skills, self-esteem, and hope.

This research can be significant for family, church, school, and community. The assets provide guidelines for the direction and purpose of educational ministry. *Funtastic Family Nights* is designed to be a way that congregations can work with families to promote these developmental assets.

All Types of Families

Families come in all sizes, shapes, and configurations. *Funtastic Family Nights* provides resources to help all families reflect, share, and dialog about God's Word as a way to build healthy family relationships.

Families with Teenagers and Younger Children

These *Funtastic Family Nights* events are aimed primarily at families with children ages 6 to 12. The activities and discussions can, however, be used to build relationships in all families. Families with children under eight may want to provide alternative activities for younger members. For each session, you might provide coloring materials or small toys and/or tabletop games. Allow families to choose alternative activities when they feel they are necessary. You will want to encourage families to include younger children in as many activities as possible. Younger children are an important part of the family system. Even when the discussion seems "over their heads," they are picking up important messages and gaining insight into their place and role in the family.

Some helpful resources to have include activity books, picture books, and a few quiet toys. Concordia Publishing House offers a wide variety of activity books for all age levels, including coloring books and products with simple paper and pencil activities. Ask your church office for the most recent Concordia catalog or visit your local Christian bookstore for specific information on available resources.

Flexible Church Events

This resource allows congregations to sponsor family "table talk" events. These events work best as 90-minute sessions. They can, however, be adapted for use during a Sunday school hour. The events also might be used in combination for a weekend retreat.

Each event includes the following components. Complete descriptions of each element begin on page 10.

- Presession Activities
- Presenting the Theme
- Individual Family Table Talk
- Closing
- Family Devotional Take-home Pages

The Core Concepts of *Funtastic Family Nights*

Christian family relationships are founded on the relationship with Jesus Christ

Dear friends, let us love one another, for love comes from God. Everyone who loves has been born of God and knows God. Whoever does not love does not know God, because God is love. (1 John 4:7–8)

The old and new covenant

The Old Testament family centered on the father. The faithful father became a reflection of God's relationship to His people. In response to the father's love, the members of the household were expected to honor and respect the father as they would the heavenly Father. This family "covenant" created a sense of loyalty, justice, and commitment among the members of the family. Jesus affirmed the love of the earthly father but expanded the understanding of the family. In the family of the "new covenant," the commitment of faith became central to God's purpose. Jesus pointed to God's loving and giving attitude that was revealed in the clearest way in Jesus

Christ. The attitude of unconditional love became the foundation of the Christian family. "Which of you, if his son asks for bread, will give him a stone? Or if he asks for a fish, will give him a snake?" (Matthew 7:9–10).

New covenant marriage

Christian marriage also is based on God's unconditional love in Jesus. It calls for men and women to give themselves in servanthood to each other. Marriage under the "new covenant" is a reflection of Christ's self-giving love for the church. "Husbands, love your wives, just as Christ loved the church and gave Himself up for her to make her holy, cleansing her by the washing with water through the word, and to present her to Himself as a radiant church, without stain or wrinkle or any other blemish, but holy and blameless. In this same way, husbands ought to love their wives as their own bodies. He who loves his wife loves himself. After all, no one ever hated his own body, but he feeds and cares for it, just as Christ does the church—for we are members of His body" (Ephesians 5:25–30). The marriage relationship of men and women is transformed as they participate in the self-giving love of Christ.

New covenant children

For people of the new covenant, children offer an opportunity for parents to be partners with God as they help their children to become children of God. The focus of the parent/child relationship is on love, honor, and respect, as well as on discipline and instruction. "Children, obey your parents in the Lord, for this is right. 'Honor your father and mother'—which is the first commandment with a promise—'that it may go well with you and that you may enjoy long life on the earth.' Fathers, do not exasperate your children; instead, bring them up in the training and instruction of the Lord" (Ephesians 6:1–4).

The purpose of a family

A fundamental purpose of the Christian family is to give witness to the love of God.

Families do that as they demonstrate what it means to be in a saving relationship with God through Jesus Christ and a part of the larger family of God. "Consequently, you are no longer foreigners and aliens, but fellow citizens with God's people and members of God's household" (Ephesians 2:19). The function of the family as a place of physical/emotional nurture is secondary in the New Testament to the primary purpose of the family of God—the nurture of faith.

Building a spiritually healthy family

A helpful model for strengthening the Christian family structure comes from Virginia Satir, a pioneer in family therapy. She identifies four basic elements of family life that can become indicators of how spiritual health is growing in a family. Every design in this manual will accent these four aspects in some way.

1. Self-worth: the feelings and ideas one has about oneself.

2. Communication: the methods we use to interact with one another.

3. The Family System: the unwritten rules that describe how family members should feel and act.

4. The Link to Society: the way family members relate to other people and institutions outside the family.

(Satir, Virginia. *The New Peoplemaking.* Palo Alto: Science and Behavior Books, Inc., 1988).

These four aspects of family life have been identified by many professionals inside and outside the church as the "core competencies" for family well-being. These elements fit our Christian model as well.

1. *Self-worth.* Every person carries a fundamental attitude toward self that is either positive or negative. Which it is becomes an important question for the health of the individual. Some families foster a sense of negative self-worth. These families seem to foster feelings of guilt and regret. Through constant negative feed-

back, they keep members thinking and feeling poorly about themselves. Even Christian families can fail to deliver positive feedback. But in those situations, family members can remember that the self-worth of a Christian is graciously connected to nothing less than the death and resurrection of Jesus Christ. "This is love: not that we loved God, but that He loved us and sent His Son as an atoning sacrifice for our sins" (1 John 4:10). By grace and through faith, I am a child of God and an inheritor of God's eternal blessing. My worth and value have been elevated beyond the angels; I am a brother or sister to Christ. What can be a greater cause for positive self-esteem? Parents who recognize their own value, especially their value in God's eyes, can communicate a sense of self-worth to their children as they depend on the power of God to love freely and unconditionally. Within such a positive family environment, members see one another as valuable to God and, therefore, of worth to each other and to the world.

2. *Communication.* All people communicate. The question is how and what happens as a result of that communication? Some families communicate poorly. They send indirect messages that are often vague and have an indistinct meaning. Such communication is neither honest nor fair. When Christians communicate, they have been called to seek the truth in love. They strive to keep no secrets, no hiding, no manipulation of the thoughts and feelings of others. Christians model their communication after their Savior, Jesus, who spoke the truth in love. Paul gives a wonderful model for communication that fosters spiritual health. "Therefore each of you must put off falsehood and speak truthfully to his neighbor, for we are members of one body. 'In your anger do not sin': Do not let the sun go down while you are still angry, and do not give the devil a foothold. He who has been stealing must steal no longer, but must

work, doing something useful with his own hands, that he may have something to share with those in need. Do not let any unwholesome talk come out of your mouths, but only what is helpful for building others up according to their needs, that it may benefit those who listen" (Ephesians 4:25–29).

3. *Rules.* Everyone follows rules. The question is what kind of rules and how well do they work for her or him? Some families establish rules that are rigid, inhuman, nonnegotiable, and unchanging. Inflexible rules that suppress the individual can be emotionally and spiritually destructive. But Christians are called to live in the freedom of the Gospel. The good news of God's forgiving love in Jesus forms the foundation for the family's "rules." Such a foundation results in rules that are established and followed because of mutual love and respect for one another as the members of the family together follow Christ's love. The rules are flexible and appropriate for the changing needs of the family.

4. *Linked to society.* Everyone is linked to society. The question is in what way and what are the results? Some families fear the "outside" world. They pull back from society and see it as a threat. They tend to blame outside forces for their problems. But Christian families see the "world" as redeemed and loved by God. Members can be encouraged to move freely into society with confidence and love. They are able to make personal choices about the world based on shared Christian values.

The family, not the church, is primarily responsible for nurturing the faith

God has placed the responsibility for nurturing children on the family. Nurture—physical and spiritual—is a basic right and privilege of the family. The church plays a role in faith formation, yet it is the family where faith is lived and acted upon. The truths and values taught and lived in the family become foundational for children as they grow. For that reason, the family, not the church, has the greatest impact on the nurture and development of faith. The activities in this book are based on the assumption that Christian education is not something done by the church but by the family assisted by the church. Such a shift in understanding may require some rethinking on the part of both family members and church leaders.

Parents are "in charge" of shaping the children entrusted to them. Christian parents must take primary responsibility to "infaith"— to live and communicate the faith to their families. Adults in the family create the opportunity for Christian development. To say it negatively, the education and youth ministries of the congregation do not have the influence of the home on the development of children. Listen to St. Paul's words to young Timothy.

> **Paul, an apostle of Christ Jesus by the will of God, according to the promise of life that is in Christ Jesus,**
> **To Timothy, my beloved son:**
> **Grace, mercy and peace from God the Father and Christ Jesus our Lord.**
> **I thank God, whom I serve, as my forefathers did, with a clear conscience, as night and day I constantly remember you in my prayers. Recalling your tears, I long to see you, so that I may be filled with joy. I have been reminded of your sincere faith, which first lived in your grandmother Lois and in your mother Eunice and, I am persuaded, now lives in you also. ... But as for you, continue in what you have learned and have become convinced of, because you know those from whom you learned it, and how from infancy you have known the holy Scriptures, which are able to make you wise for salvation through faith in Christ Jesus. All Scripture is God-breathed and is useful for teaching, rebuking, correcting and**
> **training in righteousness, so that the man of God may be thoroughly equipped for every good work.**
> **(2 Timothy 1:1–5, 3:14–17)**

Doing the Family Nights Effectively

The coordinator/facilitator

These events will work best if an individual or small group takes responsibility to coordinate the planning, scheduling, resourcing, and advertising of all the events. Each event will work best if there is one facilitator who leads the activities and helps the group move through the event. A family might take a turn facilitating an event as long as a coordinator supports their leadership and helps them understand their leadership responsibilities.

The strategy

The *Funtastic Family Nights* events are designed to encourage the interaction of people on many different levels. The primary focus, however, is family "faith talk." For that reason the family groups will spend significant time together. The events also allow time for individuals to reflect and learn on their own. And the gathering of families into a large group will reinforce learned concepts and help all participants celebrate the importance of family.

To make the various activities most effective, the coordinator/facilitator will seek to create an atmosphere of openness and acceptance in the large group. This open atmosphere will help the family small groups focus and encourage them in their sharing. These events invite participants to live out their calling to be a community of families in Christ. That living community can provide the model and encouragement for individual families to live out their faith calling.

Repetition

Each of the *Funtastic Family Nights* (except the last—which is a list of outdoor activities for families) follows a similar pattern. This pattern will help everyone become familiar with a method of gathering and sharing. Both children and adults find comfort in routine and look forward to familiar activities. The familiar pattern also can encourage families to take greater and greater ownership in the success of the event. At first the families will be highly dependent on the facilitator. After several events the families will be able to anticipate and make the process fit their way of working together. As facilitator, you should move toward sharing more and more of the leadership roles as the families become familiar with the pattern of activities.

Doing the Events

Presession Activities

Presession activities are critical for a successful event. They create an atmosphere of openness and acceptance and make everyone feel included. You will want to give everyone something to do as you greet them. Letting people mill around as they wait for everyone to arrive doesn't promote an atmosphere for learning and growth. Make sure you arrive early and have all materials and handouts ready. If you have a lot of setup work to do, you might invite several families to come early and help prepare the room. Certainly music and decorations will help create a welcoming environment.

Presenting the Theme

As facilitator, it is your responsibility to introduce the theme of each event. Usually this is done in a large group activity. In some cases, however, you will need to make a formal presentation. In either case, you will want to become familiar with the material and be prepared to lead without too much dependence on the manual.

Individual Family Table Talk

This is the heart of each event. There are reproducible handouts designed for family discussions. During family table talk, you will want to avoid interruption. Yet the role of facilitator is critical during the family table talk. In preparation for facilitating the *Funtastic Family Nights* handout, as facilitator you should do the following:

- Read the handout carefully until you are clear about the instructions and procedures for discussion.
- Highlight the main theme of the handout.
- Encourage family members to listen to one another without interrupting one another.
- Make clear how long everyone has for each section of the handout.
- Keep track of the time for the table talk handout. The times given in this manual are only suggestions. Families will require different amounts of time to complete the activities. Encourage all families to stay on task. Observe how they are doing. Make time adjustments and keep things moving.
- Announce the time when only two or three minutes remain to complete a section of the handout.
- Be available to answer questions for individual families. If you find that several families have the same question, you might want to make a general announcement to the entire group.

Ordinarily you also will need to provide materials to be used by the family groups during this time.

Closing

Most of the closings include prayer and/or music. Be sure to recruit someone if you do not feel comfortable leading the music. There are resources available from Concordia for taped sing-along music. The music suggestions in this manual are a beginning point. You should substitute according to your own musical taste and resources.

Family Devotional Take-home Page

Each event also includes a reproducible "take-home" page that families can use to continue to develop the theme. These pages can be used at the event during the table talk time, or they can be sent home for families to use as follow-up activities. If the sheets will be sent home, do not hand these out until the end of the event.

Resource Table

Gather all the needed materials for the "table talk" on one resource table. When families begin their activities, they can send a representative to get the needed supplies. This is another way to involve children in the project. It also will save time for you in preparation.

Add Food to *Funtastic Family Nights*

You can provide food at *Funtastic Family Nights* events to add fellowship and fun. Include the entire family in the food-sharing experience. Invite children to work with adults to serve or help prepare the food. Here are some food suggestions.

- Provide cookie cutters to cut shapes out of bread and make sandwiches.
- Spread cream cheese on bread or toast. Decorate with dried fruit, nuts, or colorful cereal.
- Celery with peanut butter or cream cheese and raisins is always a favorite.
- Toothpicks are fun tools for cut fruits, luncheon meats, pickles, vegetables, and cheeses.
- Use waffles to make sandwiches with fillers such as eggs, jelly, peanut butter, or breakfast meats.
- Make ice-cream sundaes with low-fat frozen yogurt.
- Find a good recipe for fortune cookies. Have everyone prepare the notes and cookies one week. The next week, distribute them to a nursing home or retirement community.

Homemade Modeling Clay

1 cup flour
1 cup water
½ cup salt
1 teaspoon vegetable oil
1 teaspoon cream of tartar

Stir all the ingredients together in a pot over medium heat. Continue stirring until the mixture forms a ball. Remove from heat and let cool. When cool, knead. Store clay in an airtight container.

The Room Setup

Prepare the room to function as a multi-purpose environment. Most of the activities could use the setup as shown. All family activities in *Funtastic Family Nights* will be conducted at the tables. As a rule you can plan four to five chairs for each table. See below for one possible room setup.

Room setup

1 What Is Your Name?

Key Concept

Names are important. God loved us enough to tell us His name and gave His Son the name Jesus. Jesus means Savior. While good names can build up, bad names also can be powerful—they can hurt.

Bible Passages

Isaiah 9:6–7
Philippians 2:5–10

Objective

Participants will reflect on their own names and how the naming process happened in their family. They will discover some of the names for Jesus. Families will discuss how to build self-esteem through communication that features positive naming. In the activities, the name of Jesus will be praised.

Materials Checklist

☐ A large sheet of butcher paper or newsprint, approximately 72″ × 36″

☐ Markers

☐ Adhesive name tags with the names or pictures of people from the Bible and the Bible reference

☐ Copies of the Family Event Handout (one for each participant)

☐ Name card—tie a string through the holes provided

☐ Copies of the Take-home Page (one for each participating family)

As Participants Arrive—Cross Names Puzzle

Post a large sheet of butcher paper or newsprint, approximately 72″ × 36″, on a wall. Title the paper "Crossing Our Names." Cross the name Jesus Christ (as shown on the next page) in big letters in the middle of the paper. As participants arrive, invite them to use a marker to write their names crossing the letters of Jesus' name as well as one another's names. Parents of small children can write their names and show them how they are connected.

```
        J
        e
Christ
        u
        s
```

Opening Prayer

Invite a young child to rehearse and then read the opening prayer. Or invite everyone to join in the prayer.

> **Dear God, today we thank You for our names. We are glad that You let us know Your name. Because Your name is Savior, our names are connected to each other forever. In Jesus' name we give thanks and pray. Amen.**

For Starters—The Name Game

Make the following points to the entire group:

- Names are important. It is difficult to have a relationship with others until you learn their names.
- God told Moses His name and that became the beginning of a special relationship between God and the people of Israel.
- There are many names for Jesus. They help us better understand who He is.
- Bad names are powerful too. Name calling can hurt.

Announce that you are going to play a name game. Each person will have the name of a person from the Bible stuck on his or her back. The goal of this game is to guess the name of the person on your back. The only way to identify the Bible character is to ask other people questions. Participants may only ask a person one question, and the answer can only be yes, no, or I don't know. Move around the room until everyone has guessed the name on their back. Or after three minutes, ask the families to return to their tables and help one another learn their names. Look up the Bible passages to help remember the characters.

Have adhesive name tags with the names of people from the Bible and the Bible reference ready for the game. Here are some possibilities (repeat them if you need more for your group). Remember that children and people with little biblical background will be at a disadvantage in this activity. Be careful to give them easy names and give them extra clues, if necessary. Do all you can to avoid embarrassing anyone.

Adam (Genesis 2:19–20)
Eve (Genesis 3:20)
Methuselah (Genesis 5:27)
Noah (Genesis 7:6)
Abraham (Genesis 17:3–5)
Sarah (Genesis 17:15)
Isaac (Genesis 17:19)
Rebekah (Genesis 25:20)
Esau (Genesis 25:25)
Jacob (Genesis 28:10–13)
Rachel (Genesis 29:16–20)
Joseph (Genesis 37:3)
Moses (Exodus 2:5–10)
Miriam (Exodus 15:19–21)
Joshua (Joshua 1:1; 24:25)
Samson (Judges 16:6–9)
Delilah (Judges 16:6–9)
Ruth (Ruth 1:15–19)
Samuel (1 Samuel 2:26)
David (1 Samuel 17:48–51)
Solomon (1 Kings 4:29–30)
Elijah (2 Kings 2:8–12)
Daniel (Daniel 6:16–22)
Jonah (Jonah 1:15–17)
Job (Job 1:7–12)

Esther (Esther 2:15–16)
Isaiah (Isaiah 1:1)
Matthew (Matthew 9:9)
John the Baptizer (Matthew 3:1–3)
Peter (Matthew 14:26–30)
Saul/Paul (Acts 9:3–8; 13:9)
Zacchaeus (Luke 19:1–5)
Elizabeth (Luke 1:13)
Mary (Luke 2:30–35)
Timothy (Acts 16:1–3)
Nicodemus (John 3:1–4)
Barnabas (Acts 12:25–13:3)

Handout Facilitation Suggestions

Ask the groups to send one person to gather the necessary materials from the supply table at the appropriate time. Remind them that even if smaller children may not respond to the questions, they will grow from being a part of the family discussion.

Give a copy of the handout to each person at the tables. Instruct them to respond to the questions and activities. Keep groups aware of the time and encourage them to move on to each portion of the handout.

Closing

Gather in a large circle, families standing together. One person in the family will introduce the other family members one at a time, using their full name in the pattern that follows. Continue until all families have been introduced.

Family Leader: I am (first name, middle name, last name).

Group: Jesus loves you (first name), and so do we.

Family Leader: This is (full name of another family member).

Group: Jesus loves you (first name), and so do we.

Sing "Kids of the Kingdom." (See *All God's People Sing!* 150.)

Play a recording of Handel's *Messiah,* "For Unto Us a Child Is Born." Invite everyone to listen for the names of Jesus.

Pass out the Take-home Page as families leave.

What Is Your Name?

Focus (5 minutes)

The prophet Isaiah foretells the coming of the Messiah. When a baby is born, you give it a name. Work together to underline the names for the baby boy that will be born.

For to us a child is born,
to us a son is given,
and the government will be on His
shoulders.
And He will be called
Wonderful Counselor, Mighty God,
Everlasting Father, Prince of Peace.
Of the increase of His government and peace
there will be no end.
He will reign on David's throne
and over His kingdom,
establishing and upholding it
with justice and righteousness
from that time on and forever.
The zeal of the Lord *Almighty*
will accomplish this.
(Isaiah 9:6–7)

Activity— Name Acronym (10 minutes)

Collect the materials from the supply table—enough for each person to make a name card. Write a descriptive word for each letter in your name. (See the example for "Kurt.") Color and decorate your name card. Tie a string through the holes provided so you can wear the card. Older family members can help younger children write the words. Even little ones can color and decorate it. Continue decorating your name card as you move on to the discussion starters.

Kite
Understanding
River
Talkative

Discussion—The Story of How You Got Your Name (15 minutes)

Do you have a pet or a toy that you have named? What name did you give it and why?

Each person around the table tells how they got their own name. Parents can supply needed detail.

If you were named after someone, who was it, and why was that person important to those who named you?

If you had been born the opposite sex, what would you have been named?

What other names were thought of for you?

If you know a meaning or the origin of your name, share that and say why it is important for you.

Closing (5 minutes)

Jesus said, "I tell you the truth, My Father will give you whatever you ask in My name" (John 16:23). That is why we pray in the name of Jesus.

What do you feel or think when you hear the name Jesus? How do you feel when someone uses Jesus' name without respect? Go around the table and give everyone a chance to share. Remember it is okay to pass.

What Is Your Name?

Bible Reading

Your attitude should be the same as that of
*   Christ Jesus:*
Who, being in very nature God,
*   did not consider equality with God some-*
*   thing to be grasped,*
but made Himself nothing,
*   taking the very nature of a servant,*
*   being made in human likeness.*
And being found in appearance as a man,
*   He humbled Himself*
*   and became obedient to death—even death*
*   on a cross!*
Therefore God exalted Him to the highest place
*   and gave Him the name that is above*
*   every name,*
that at the name of Jesus every knee
*   should bow,*
*   in heaven and on earth and under the earth.*
(Philippians 2:5–10)

Family Time—
In the Name of Love

You can do things to hurt one another and you can say things to help one another. In this exercise you will practice what to say when someone does a hurtful or unacceptable thing. Make a large chart like the one below and invite everyone to participate in the discussion. Remember, even children who do not yet read can benefit from seeing you write their words and listening to the discussion.

What They Do	What Not to Say	A Better Way
Speaking loudly	You are a loudmouth.	You are talking so loud it is uncomfortable for me.
Loudly slurp	Don't be a slob.	You are slurping loud enough to be heard over our conversation.
Pushes other child	Stop being a bully.	When you push your sister/brother, it makes me afraid that she/he will be hurt.

Reflection

Sticks and stones may break my bones, but names can break my spirit.

The name of Jesus is wonderful to our ears because of who Jesus is and what Jesus did. How does your name sound to you? If it sounds wonderful to you, it is because you have been given love, encouragement, and forgiveness. When the sound of your own name feels less than wonderful, it might be because you have received lots of criticism, condemnation, or ridicule.

Many of the verbal put-downs happen in the family when we make judgments about the behavior of others. As a family, you can work to transform your communication from hurting to helping simply by describing what you can see and hear rather than making a judgment or calling a name.

Unacceptable behavior should not be ignored. But you can save one another's self-esteem if you simply describe what you see someone doing or saying in simple, basic, accurate terms. Use the family time below to practice this communication skill.

Prayer Time

Think of a time in your family when you were arguing and calling one another names and speaking critically of one another. Then complete this prayer sentence. Go around the room and invite everyone to share their prayer.

Dear heavenly Father, thank You for my name _____. Help me to speak kinder words when _____. In Jesus' name. Amen.

funtastic family nights

2
It's about Time

Key Concept

Jesus came to establish His reign (kingdom) in our lives. Jesus invites us to repent and believe the good news. These concepts are foundational for developing family relationships.

Bible Passage

Mark 1:14–15

Objective

The purpose is to invite families to discuss their use of time and to recognize that it is always time to repent and say, "I'm sorry."

Materials Checklist

- ☐ Large clock with a second hand or a large digital clock with seconds
- ☐ Name tags and markers
- ☐ Two large signs (see instructions in For Starters)
- ☐ Sheet of poster board (one for each family table)
- ☐ Crayons or markers
- ☐ Copies of the Family Event Handout (one for each participant)
- ☐ Copies of the Take-home Page (one for each participating family)

As Participants Arrive— Clock In

Family Name	First Name	Exact Time

Display a large clock with a second hand or a large digital clock with seconds next to a poster-size sign-in page (see previous page). You can make the poster using newsprint or poster board, or you can write it on a chalkboard.

Have name tags and markers for everyone to wear to display their first names. Parents can make name tags for children who cannot yet print their names.

Ask each family system to be seated at a table.

Opening Prayer

Invite the entire group to pray with you.

Dear heavenly Father, You sent Jesus to live here on earth and spend time with people. We praise Him for He is eternal, yet He chose to be with us in time so He could restore our hope of eternal life. Send Your Spirit to help us be time conscious and responsible in our use of time. Amen.

For Starters

Ask the large group:

What is your favorite time of day? Are you a morning person or an evening person?

Post two large signs on either side of the room as follows:

My favorite time of the day is MORNING.

My favorite time of the day is EVENING.

Instruct everyone to stand by the sign that best describes them. If small children are different from their parents, try to entrust them to someone in that group, but only if they are comfortable going there.

Ask participants to stay on their side of the room and form small buzz groups (three to four people) and discuss the following for one minute:

What do you like about your time of day?

Now discuss for another minute:

What is difficult to understand about the people on the other side of the room?

In the large group, ask for comments from both sides, alternating back and forth, to this question:

What observations would you like to make about the people on the other side?

Take five or six comments, thanking people for their observations. Ask everyone to return to their tables.

Handout Facilitation Suggestions

Ask the groups to send one person to gather the necessary materials from the supply table at the appropriate time. Remind them that even if smaller children may not respond to the questions, they will grow from being a part of the family discussion.

Give a copy of the handout to each person at the tables. Instruct them to respond to the questions and activities. Keep groups aware of the time and encourage them to move on to each portion of the handout.

Closing

Form a large circle and hold hands. Sing one stanza of a familiar children's song.

Pass out the Take-home Page as families leave.

It's about Time

Focus (5 minutes)

Give everyone at the table a chance to answer the following question:

> **Which timely phrase do you think is used most often in your home?**

It's time to get up.
It's time to go to bed.
It's time to eat.
It's time to take out the garbage.
It's time to say your prayers.
other _____

Activity—How Long? (10 minutes)

Time one another on the following tasks. Ask different children to do different tasks so it is not a competition against one another. Assign the tasks according to appropriate age level. Give a child the responsibility of keeping time. Before each task, ask everyone to guess how long it will take to complete the task.

- Give everyone at the table a hug.
- Sing one stanza of "Jesus Loves Me."
- Untie and tie your shoes.
- Read the Bible passage in the Focus section.

Activity—I'm Sorry Poster (15 minutes)

Make an "I'm Sorry" poster. Draw a picture of your family at a time when saying "I'm sorry" would be the right thing to do. The poster might be a collage of small drawings.

 Use the poster board and crayons or markers to draw the picture. Be sure to involve everyone in the creation.

Focus (10 minutes)

Read the following passage and statement at your table and give everyone a chance to respond to the question that follows.

> After John was put in prison, Jesus went into Galilee, proclaiming the good news of God. "The time has come," He said. "The kingdom of God is near. Repent and believe the good news!" *(Mark 1:14–15)*

> It's time. You probably hear that at your home a lot: It's time to go to school. It's time to get up. It's time to eat. Do you ever hear, "It's time to repent"? When Jesus came to talk with people, He said, "It is time to repent." He meant that people should look into their hearts and seek God's help to admit that they have hurt others and offended God and are sorry for the things they have done.

When are some times in your family that you need to say, "It's time for me to repent"?

Closing—The Kingdom Is at Hand (5 minutes)

Hold hands and take turns responding to the following statement:

> **Jesus is always with us, and a time when Jesus was very close to our family was when ...**

Take-home PAGE

It's about Time

Bible Reading

At once the Spirit sent Him out into the desert, and He was in the desert forty days, being tempted by Satan. He was with the wild animals, and angels attended Him.

After John was put in prison, Jesus went into Galilee, proclaiming the good news of God. "The time has come," He said. "The kingdom of God is near. Repent and believe the good news!"

As Jesus walked beside the Sea of Galilee, He saw Simon and his brother Andrew casting a net into the lake, for they were fishermen. "Come follow Me," Jesus said, "and I will make you fishers of men." At once they left their nets and followed Him.
(Mark 1:12–18)

Family Time

Being on time is important in family life. There are times when getting someplace puts stress on family relationships. Take some time now, when there is no pressure, to go somewhere and talk about this timely topic.

Recall a recent time when you all had to go somewhere. How would you respond to the following questions? It is not important that you agree with one another's responses. It is very important, however, that you listen and try to understand one another.

- Who is the first to be ready to go?
- Who reminds everyone of how much time is left?
- How do you feel when you are late?
- If being on time is important to you, why is it important?

Remember, this discussion is meant to lead to better awareness and understanding. If anyone becomes "heated," stop the exercise and reschedule it for another time.

Prayer Time

Say the introductory phrase and read the Bible passage as a prayer.

> <u>Lord, help us to plan our time wisely.</u>
> For there is a time for everything,
> and a season for every activity
>   under heaven:
> a time to be born and a time to die,
> a time to plant and a time to uproot,
> a time to kill and a time to heal,
> a time to tear down and a time to build,
> a time to weep and a time to laugh,
> a time to mourn and a time to dance,
> a time to scatter stones and a time
>   to gather them,
> a time to embrace and a time to refrain,
> a time to search and a time to give up,
> a time to keep and a time to throw away,
> a time to tear and a time to mend,
> a time to be silent and a time to speak,
> a time to love and a time to hate,
> a time for war and a time for peace.
> (Ecclesiastes 3:1–8)

funtastic family nights

3
Pray for One Another

Key Concept

Prayer is an expression of trust and faith in God. Families pray together as a response to God's command and as a way to affirm their spiritual connection with God and with one another.

Bible Passages

Psalm 141
James 5:13–16
1 Peter 5:7

Objective

Participants will experience opportunities to pray together as families and as the gathered church. They will be given practical ideas for fostering spontaneous prayer life in their homes.

Materials Checklist

☐ Strips of construction paper 1″ × 8½″

☐ Stapler and staples

☐ Incense with holder or ashtray

☐ Standing altar cross

☐ Candles

☐ Matches

☐ Name tags and markers

☐ Four index cards of different colors for each participant (white, green, yellow, blue). You may adapt the colors to what is available.

☐ Copies of the Family Event Handout (one for each participant)

☐ Copies of the Take-home Page (one for each participating family)

As Participants Arrive— Prayer Chain

Prepare an altar. Use a table with a cross and candles. Include some incense in an incense holder or ashtray.

Ask everyone to prepare a name tag. Then invite everyone to add to a prayer chain.

Using strips of construction paper and markers, encourage everyone to write down their prayer concerns. Then staple the strips of paper into a loop, making the links of a "prayer chain" on the altar. The prayer chain should start at the base of the cross and drape across the altar. This chain also will be used in the closing.

For Starters—"Mother, May I?"

Gather the participants at the tables and invite everyone to play "Mother, May I?" Remind them that they can do whatever you tell them to do, but only if they ask, "Mother, may I?" and you respond "Yes, you may." Here are some examples:

Stand up.

Clap three times.

Shout amen.

Wiggle your nose.

Hop on one foot.

Wink at two people

Hug a friend.

Sit down.

Opening Prayer

Light the candles and the incense on the altar. Announce that this family event will focus on prayer. Prayer is much more than "Mother, May I?" It is our loving communication with God our Father. As you read the following psalm, encourage participants to lift up their hands in prayer when they smell the incense. (Demonstrate with hands extended above your shoulders, palms up). Pray together:

O LORD, I call to You; come quickly to me.
Hear my voice when I call to You.
May my prayer be set before You like incense;
may the lifting up of my hands be like the evening sacrifice.
Set a guard over my mouth, O LORD;
keep watch over the door of my lips.
Let not my heart be drawn to what is evil,
to take part in wicked deeds

With men who are evildoers;
let me not eat of their delicacies.
Let a righteous man strike me—it is a kindness;
let him rebuke me—it is oil on my head.
My head will not refuse it. ...
But my eyes are fixed on You, O Sovereign LORD;
in You I take refuge—do not give me over to death.
Keep me from the snares they have laid for me,
from the traps set by evildoers.
Let the wicked fall into their own nets,
while I pass by in safety. Amen. (Psalm 141)

Handout Facilitation Suggestions

Ask the groups to send one person to gather the necessary materials from the supply table at the appropriate time. Remind them that even if smaller children may not respond to the questions, they will grow from being a part of the family discussion.

Give a copy of the handout to each person at the tables. Instruct them to respond to the questions and activities. Keep groups aware of the time and encourage them to move on to each portion of the handout.

Closing

Gather the participants in a semicircle ending at the two corners of the altar. Take the prayer chain from the altar and give it to the people on each end to hold. Ask everyone to join hands. Sing one stanza of "What a Friend We Have in Jesus." Invite each family to pray the prayer they wrote at their table. Then sing another stanza of the hymn or of a song of your choice.

Pass out the Take-home Page as families leave.

Pray for One Another

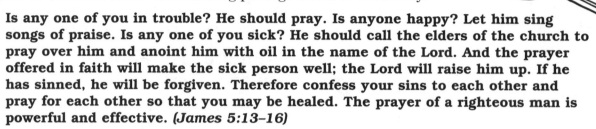

Focus (15 minutes)

As you gather as a family, ask each person to add to a family prayer list. Go around the table and share your prayer thoughts. Think about those prayers as someone reads the following passage aloud to the family.

Is any one of you in trouble? He should pray. Is anyone happy? Let him sing songs of praise. Is any one of you sick? He should call the elders of the church to pray over him and anoint him with oil in the name of the Lord. And the prayer offered in faith will make the sick person well; the Lord will raise him up. If he has sinned, he will be forgiven. Therefore confess your sins to each other and pray for each other so that you may be healed. The prayer of a righteous man is powerful and effective. *(James 5:13–16)*

Activity (15 minutes)

There are four index cards on your table. Write a word, draw a picture, or design a symbol for a prayer on each of the cards according to the following directions.

- The white card is for prayers of confession of sins.

- The green card is for your physical needs.

- The yellow card is for your spiritual needs.

- The blue card is for prayers of praise and thanksgiving to God.

Go around to each member. Use the cards to take turns speaking a prayer. Repeat the process until all have had a chance to pray. Then take the cards and place them on the altar.

Discuss the following prayer stem and complete it as a family. Choose someone who will read it in the large group for closing.

Dear Jesus, our family offers this prayer in the presence of our friends and neighbors ...

Pray for One Another

Bible Reading

Cast all your anxiety on Him because He cares for you.
(1 Peter 5:7)

Reflection

Some people suggest that the best way to pray is with the Bible open before us. The open Bible is a way of completing the communication loop. We speak to God through prayer. God speaks to us through His Word. All families need to find time to pray for and with each other. Simple children's prayers are a good way to begin a life of prayer. These can give way to prayers that arise from our needs, our experiences, and our faith. Prayer is a good habit. Like all good habits we need to practice it over and over again. Children can develop a rich prayer life as adults model their own dependence on God and prayer.

One way to teach a child how prayer is connected to life is to conclude a conversation with prayer. No matter what the discussion is about, prayer can be a way of moving what was said into the context of our relationship with God. A parent and child discussing a difficult class in school could end the conversation by praying for the teacher, the school, and the students. Then they might give God thanks for minds to think and the years of education that are still before them.

Put prayer time into your daily schedule.

Family Prayer Time

It may take time to develop a conversational style of prayer. The following prayer stems may be used for family prayer. Ask each family member to choose two or three prayer stems from the list below. Give them time to think about these prayer starters or even write them down. Then go around the circle and ask each person to speak the prayers out loud. The leader can then end the prayer with the Lord's Prayer or a song.

- **Help me when I am afraid of …**
- **Be with my friend _____ because …**
- **I am looking forward to …**
- **Thank You for …**
- **I am worried about …**
- **I have a tough time ahead…**
- **Show me the way to …**
- **Forgive me when …**
- **I want to thank and praise You for …**
- **I need You, Lord, for …**
- **Please rescue …**

funtastic family nights

4
A New Spirit

Key Concept

Our human nature is sinful. God knows our condition and continues to rescue and renew us in Jesus. In our family relationships we can open our hearts to one another because we are confident of God's forgiveness in Christ. We can build healthy relationships that are founded on God's mercy and the freedom of the Gospel.

Bible Passage

Psalm 51:5–13

Objective

Participants will be encouraged to celebrate their relationship with the merciful heavenly Father who knows us and loves us in Jesus Christ. This event also will give families an opportunity to open their hearts to one another as a way to build strong relationships in the family.

Materials Checklist

☐ Name tags and markers

☐ Tape or CD player

☐ A large heart attached to a sheet of newsprint or poster board—to be posted on the wall. Title the heart "The Family of God."

☐ 11" × 17" paper for each participant

☐ Red construction paper, one sheet for everyone

☐ Masking tape

☐ Glue (a bottle or stick for each table)

☐ Magazines with pictures of people in a variety of situations

☐ Copies of the Family Event Handout (one for each participant)

☐ Copies of the Take-home Page (one for each participating family)

As Participants Arrive—The Family of God

Play background music on a tape player or CD player. On a wall, post a large heart attached to a sheet of newsprint or poster board. Title the heart "The Family of God." Invite everyone to make a name tag. Adults can help younger children. Invite everyone to sign in on the large heart on the wall.

Opening Prayer

Dear heavenly Father, we come together to seek Your guidance for our family. Remind us of our need for You. Restore to us the joy of salvation through Your Son, Jesus, and send Your free Spirit to strengthen us for holy living. Amen.

For Starters—Have a Heart

Instruct each family group to be seated at a table. Ask each person to make a "heart card." Use 11″ × 17″ paper. Fold the paper in half to make a four-sided card (8½″ × 11″). Draw a heart on red construction paper and tear it out. Glue the construction paper heart onto the card. Write your name on the cover (front page) with a marker. Assist younger children with the task.

Encourage everyone to tear out pictures or words from magazines that represent things about themselves that almost everybody knows. Glue them to the front of the heart card. Parents can help younger children prepare their cards.

When everyone has completed a card, ask everyone to take their cards and stand in a large circle. Infants can be in the arms of a parent while toddlers can be part of the circle. Tell every other person to take two steps into the circle. You should now have two concentric circles. Tell participants that as long as the music plays, they should walk in a circle—the inside circle going clockwise, the outside circle going counterclockwise. When the music stops, participants are to find someone in the other circle and tell them about the outside of their card until the music starts again. During the music, participants continue walking. Start and stop the music four or five times, then ask participants to return to their seats.

Handout Facilitation Suggestions

Ask the groups to send one person to gather the necessary materials from the supply table at the appropriate time. Remind them that even if smaller children may not respond to the questions, they will grow from being a part of the family discussion.

Give a copy of the handout to each person at the tables. Instruct them to respond to the questions and activities. Keep groups aware of the time and encourage them to move on to each portion of the handout.

Closing

Form a large circle and hold hands while you read the following passage as a benediction:

So then, brothers, stand firm and hold to the teachings we passed on to you, whether by word of mouth or by letter.
May our Lord Jesus Christ Himself and God our Father, who loved us and by His grace gave us eternal encouragement and good hope, encourage your hearts and strengthen you in every good deed and word. (2 Thessalonians 2:15–17)

Pass out the Take-home Page as families leave.

A New Spirit

Focus— Secret Heart (15 minutes)

Ask someone at your table to read the following passage aloud. Note the truth concerning original sin. Focus on the condition of the heart with and without God.

Surely I was sinful at birth,
sinful from the time my mother
conceived me.
Surely You desire truth in the inner parts;
You teach me wisdom in the inmost place.
Cleanse me with hyssop, and I will be clean;
wash me, and I will be whiter than snow.
Let me hear joy and gladness;
let the bones You have crushed rejoice.
Hide Your face from my sins
and blot out all my iniquity.
Create in me a pure heart, O God,
and renew a steadfast spirit within me.
Do not cast me away from Your presence
or take Your Holy Spirit from me.
Restore to me the joy of Your salvation
and grant me a willing spirit, to sustain me.
Then I will teach transgressors Your ways,
and sinners will turn back to You.
(Psalm 51:5–13)

Discuss the following questions at your table with the children participating as they are able. (Remember it is important for small children to hear your faith talk.)

What do you think is the condition of the heart with and without God?

How would you describe your "inner parts" or "inmost place"?

Note that hyssop is a small bushy plant that is well-suited as a brush. It is often used as a symbol of cleaning. What does it mean to be washed "whiter than snow" by God's grace?

Activity—Open Your Hearts (15 minutes)

Now go through the magazines again and tear out pictures or words that symbolize your inner heart before and after the cleansing you receive as God forgives your sins because of Jesus. Glue the pictures inside your heart card. Glue the "before" pictures of sin and separation on the inside left page and the "after" pictures of the clean, joyous, glad heart on the inside right page. As you complete this activity, talk with your children and explain what sin is. Sin is the actions we do that are against God's will for us. Sin is also how we are without God.

Extended—From the Heart (10 minutes)

Choose one thing from the inside of your card to share at your table. Going around the circle, ask each member to share before anyone speaks twice. It is okay to pass.

Closing—Thankful and Willing Hearts (5 minutes)

Ask the children to draw a picture of what they are thankful for on the back of their heart card. Teenagers and adults can complete the following prayer stem.

Dear heavenly Father, please give me a willing spirit so I can ...

Go around your family circle showing your pictures or reading your prayer sentences.

funtastic family nights

A New Spirit

Bible Reading

Surely I was sinful at birth,
*   sinful from the time my mother conceived me.*
Surely You desire truth in the inner parts;
*   You teach me wisdom in the inmost place.*
Cleanse me with hyssop, and I will be clean;
*   wash me, and I will be whiter than snow.*
Let me hear joy and gladness;
*   let the bones You have crushed rejoice.*
Hide Your face from my sins
*   and blot out all my iniquity.*
Create in me a pure heart, O God,
*   and renew a steadfast spirit within me.*
Do not cast me away from Your presence
*   or take Your Holy Spirit from me.*
Restore to me the joy of Your salvation
*   and grant me a willing spirit, to sustain me.*
Then I will teach transgressors Your ways,
*   and sinners will turn back to You.*
(Psalm 51:5–13)

Reflection—Self-Disclosure

Giving and receiving information about ourselves goes on all the time in families. Yet there is a lot about ourselves that we withhold from other family members. We might hide feelings, opinions, past mistakes, or other similar things. People have lots of reasons for keeping secrets. Some people may be afraid they will be made fun of; others may want to control people

When we are more open with each other, we can develop stronger and more honest relationships within the family. Some things will always remain private, but our willingness to share can help us grow closer to one another and develop trusting relationships.

Family Time—Favorite Things

Ask someone to read aloud the Bible passage listed above. Then describe what you think is in your "inmost place."

Ask everyone to get three things that are important to them. These things might come from bedrooms or anywhere in the house. They should be items that you would not sell or give away. After the items have been gathered, ask each person to tell about their "treasured things" and why they are important.

Prayer Time

Place all the items in the center of the room or on the table where you are seated and say the following prayer together:

Dear God and Savior, we thank You for these wonderful things that have given joy to our lives. We are even more thankful for the people who are part of this family. Help us to love and cherish one another. In Jesus' name we pray. Amen.

5 Tell Me a Story

Key Concept

Stories have power. They describe our sense of who we are and give meaning to our lives. Positive stories enrich our lives, while negative stories can detract from the quality of our life together. Jesus used stories to teach about the kingdom of God. In His life, death, and resurrection, we know the purpose of our story and how our story will end.

Bible Passages

Luke 10:30–37
Matthew 13:3–9

Objective

Participants will be encouraged to tell stories as a way of strengthening the bonds between family members. They will come to know that their life's story is connected to the story of Jesus.

Materials Checklist

☐ Children's storybooks and children's Bibles. Concordia offers a wide range of picture books and early reader materials based on Bible stories, including the Arch Books and Hear Me Read series.

☐ Name tags and markers

☐ Crayons and coloring paper

☐ Copies of the Family Event Handout (one for each participant)

☐ Copies of the Take-home Page (one for each participating family)

As Participants Arrive

Ask everyone to make a name tag. Have storybooks and children's Bibles available for the children to select and read. Even prereaders can enjoy picture books or books that can be read to them.

Opening Prayer

Ask a volunteer to offer a prayer for the individuals and the families present.

For Starters

Gather everyone and tell them that, with their help, you will act out a story that Jesus told. Ask for volunteers to come forward. Mix up the boys and girls, the moms and dads. Tell the actors that they will pantomime the story as you read it. You will need the following actors:

A traveler

Three or four robbers (no type-casting required)

A priest

A priest's assistant

A foreigner

The foreigner's donkey (preferably a father)

Motel owner

To prepare for the story, show the actors the location of the road that winds down the mountain. Tell the robbers to hide and be ready. Put the other actors in the order in which they will appear.

Read the story as written here, or tell the story in your own words. Pause for the described action to take place.

Handout Facilitation Suggestions

Ask the groups to send one person to gather the necessary materials from the supply table at the appropriate time. Remind them that even if smaller children may not respond to the questions, they will grow from being a part of the family discussion.

Give a copy of the handout to each person at the tables. Instruct them to respond to the questions and activities. Keep groups aware of the time and encourage them to move on to each portion of the handout.

When there are about 15 minutes left, gather participants into clusters of three or four families to give a brief review of their story.

Closing

Sing the hymn "I Love to Tell the Story." Pass out the Take-home Page as families leave.

Jesus was once asked, "Who is my neighbor?" So He told this story.

A traveler was going down from Jerusalem to Jericho when he was attacked by robbers. They stripped him of his clothes, beat him, took his money, and ran back to their seats. The audience shouted *BOO!* The robbers left the traveler half dead and moaning loudly. He moaned *LOUDLY.*

A priest happened to be going down the same road. When he saw the man, he shook his head and passed by *far* on the other side. No, *even farther* on the other side, then he went to his seat. The audience *HISSED.* So too a priest's assistant came to the place and saw the traveler. He covered his eyes and passed by *far* on the other side and went to his seat. The audience *HISSED.*

But then came a foreigner, riding on his donkey, yes, riding on his donkey as he came to where the man was. When the foreigner saw the injured man, he held his hands to his cheeks and said in a loud voice, *"Oh, my!"* Then the donkey said, *"Hee-haw!"*

The foreigner took pity on the traveler. He went to him and bandaged his wounds, pouring on oil and wine. The audience *CHEERED.* Then he put the man on his own donkey, and the donkey said, *"Oh, my!"* They took the traveler down the road to a motel, put him in a room, and made sure he was comfortable—*very comfortable.* The man took out two silver coins and gave them to the motel owner. He shook his finger right under the motel owner's nose and said, "Look after him and when I return, I will pay you for any extra expense you may have." The end.

Then all the characters stood up and took a bow. And the audience *CLAPPED* and *CHEERED.*

Then Jesus asked the question, "Which of these three do you think was a neighbor to the man who fell into the hands of robbers?" The audience replied, "The one who had mercy." Jesus told them, "Go and do likewise." *(Based on Luke 10:30–37)*

Tell Me a Story

Focus (5 minutes)

Jesus told many stories. Some of them are called parables. Parables are sometimes called earthly stories with a heavenly meaning. Listen to this parable and see if you can figure out what it means.

[Jesus said]: "Listen! A farmer went out to sow his seed. As he was scattering the seed, some fell along the path, and the birds came and ate it up. Some fell on rocky places, where it did not have much soil. It sprang up quickly, because the soil was shallow. But when the sun came up, the plants were scorched, and they withered because they had no root. Other seed fell among thorns, which grew up and choked the plants, so that they did not bear grain. Still other seed fell on good soil. It came up, grew and produced a crop, multiplying thirty, sixty, or even a hundred times." Then Jesus said, "He who has ears to hear, let him hear." *(Mark 4:3–9)*

Extended—A Family Story (15 minutes)

Parent(s), think of a story about your family that showed the hand of God at work in your life. Or describe an event you know about from the life of your parents or grandparents. See if you can find the spiritual meaning in the story. Working as a family, use the paints and brushes to paint symbols or pictures that retell the story. Make sure everyone is involved. Later you will gather in clusters of three or four families to give a brief review of the story.

Activity (15 minutes)

While children draw a picture about the story of the farmer, ask the children what they think the story means. Talk about the variety of possibilities. There are no wrong answers, just thoughts and insights.

Jesus did explain this parable later in the Bible. Listen to its meaning.

[Jesus said]: "The farmer sows the word. Some people are like seed along the path, where the word is sown. As soon as they hear it, Satan comes and takes away the word that was sown in them. Others, like seed sown on rocky places, hear the word and at once receive it with joy. But since they have no root, they last only a short time. When trouble or persecution comes because of the word, they quickly fall away. Still others, like seed sown among thorns, hear the word; but the worries of this life, the deceitfulness of wealth and the desires for other things come in and choke the word, making it unfruitful. Others, like seed sown on good soil, hear the word, accept it, and produce a crop— thirty, sixty or even a hundred times what was sown." *(Mark 4:14–20)*

Take-home PAGE

Tell Me a Story

Reflection—The Art of Storytelling

Storytelling is a skill that can contribute to the spiritual development of the family. Stories read to small children become an important part of their early learning. The bedtime story is more than a simple routine. Telling stories, especially stories about the family, is a nurturing and spiritually enriching activity. Here is a formula for practicing and perfecting the art of storytelling.

1 Think of an experience that you had when you were growing up. The event does not have to be traumatic, exciting, or terrifying. The best stories are simple slices of life that are still important to you. You may remember stories by paging though a family photo album.

2 Write down the facts: Who did what? Who said what?

3 Try to get in touch with the feelings you had when the event first occurred. Describe the way your feelings changed as the incident unfolded.

4 Think of descriptive words or images to express your feelings: "I felt safe, like having a warm blanket wrapped around me." "I felt alone, like being in a big woods all by myself." "I felt silly, like a circus clown." "I felt happy, like being at the beach when the sun goes down."

5 Think through what you learned about yourself from this experience. Identify what you learned about the others involved in the story. Try to focus the story on one key idea or concept that you learned.

6 How did this story affect you spiritually (your relationship to God, to other Christians, to the world)? Try to focus on one key idea or concept here as well.

7 Keep the story comfortably short and limit your storytelling time to only one story at a time.

The story outline

This is a story about me and how/when I learned about …

This event showed me how God was active in my life to …

Describe what happened and how you were feeling.

When the story is finished, restate what you learned.

Family Time

Schedule a time to gather for family stories. Each person can prepare a story to tell. The story should be true, and it has to be about the teller. Parent(s) can prepare a story from the suggestions above.

Gather in a special, comfortable place where there are no distractions. You may want to light candles, play soft music, or do anything that will create a comfortable atmosphere.

Prayer Time

Complete the following sentence and share it with one another:

My favorite Bible story is _____ because _____.

Parents, remember which story the children chose and be sure to tell it in the future.

6 Change

Key Concept

Change is inevitable; growth is optional. Families go through many changes in their life journey. This family night will help participants consider change in their life and see it as part of God's plan for their growth and spiritual development.

Bible Passage

Luke 2:41–52

Objective

Participants will celebrate life's changes in the light of God's unchangeable love. Family groups will reflect on changes that have happened in their lives and look for God's hand in those changes. And family leaders will consider ways to identify problems caused by change and seek ways to make change positive for the family.

Materials Checklist

- ☐ Large sheets of newsprint (one for each table)
- ☐ Tape player or CD player and cassettes or CDs
- ☐ Name tags and markers
- ☐ Crayons
- ☐ Modeling clay (see recipe on page 11)
- ☐ Copies of the Family Event Handout (one for each participant)
- ☐ Copies of the Take-home Page (one for each participating family)

As Participants Arrive

Have play dough or modeling clay out on the tables and invite everyone to begin working the clay. For starters, they might make a shape or symbol that reminds them of something that happened that day.

Opening Prayer

Read stanza 3 of the hymn "Abide with Me" and say:

Tonight we will be looking at change and growth in our families. We will celebrate the fact that Jesus will never change His love for us.

For Starters—The Object of Change

Encourage everyone to use the clay to make a model or representation of something that caused the greatest change in their family. Parents can discuss the task with young children and help them with ideas. Adults can choose to depict their family of origin or their current family.

When everyone has completed the project, tell them that they are going to play "Musical Pairs." Instruct them to take their sculpture and silently mill about while you play music. When the music stops, they are to explain their clay creation to the person closest to them.

Handout Facilitation Suggestions

Ask the groups to send one person to gather the necessary materials from the supply table at the appropriate time. Remind them that even if smaller children may not respond to the questions, they will grow from being a part of the family discussion.

Give a copy of the handout to each person at the tables. Instruct them to respond to the questions and activities. Keep groups aware of the time and encourage them to move on to each portion of the handout.

Families may need assistance getting the time line started. It might be helpful to prepare a sample time line for your own family as described in the handout. Tell the large group about it as they begin to work.

Closing

Gather the group in a large circle and invite participants to look at each person in the circle. While everyone is looking around the circle, say:

Everyone is here for a purpose; each person has contributed to the community that we experience today. We will never be exactly the same again, yet God is with us in this time and in this place. Jesus is here in each and all of us.

Invite everyone to join in the hymn "Abide with Me."

Pass out the Take-home Page as families leave.

Change

Focus (10 minutes)

Ask someone in your family to read the following passage aloud.

> When His parents saw Him, they were astonished. His mother said to Him, "Son, why have You treated us like this? Your father and I have been anxiously searching for You."
>
> "Why were you searching for Me?" He asked. "Didn't you know I had to be in My Father's house?" But they did not understand what He was saying to them.
>
> Then He went down to Nazareth with them and was obedient to them. But His mother treasured all these things in her heart. And Jesus grew in wisdom and stature, and in favor with God and men. *(Luke 2:48–52)*

Activity—Table Talk (10 minutes)

What was Mary's mood during this short event at the Jerusalem temple? (You may need to review what happened just before the encounter in the temple. Look over the verses that come before the text in your Bible.)

Read the Bible passage above again. As you do, ask the children to choose the face that best describes Mary's mood for the sentences in the text.

  afraid   dumbfounded

Extended—Your Family Time Line (15 minutes)

Everyone can participate in the completion of a time line for your family.

Lay a large sheet of newsprint across your table and use markers to draw a time line. Begin with the birth of the oldest parent and end with today's date. Measure off and mark the decades. Place all significant changes on the time line (for example, marriages, births, deaths, moves, job changes, school, etc.) and draw pictures and symbols with crayons to depict the changes.

After you have completed the major events, use different colors of crayons to graph the ups and downs of family togetherness, financial status, health, and spiritual growth along the baseline of the time line.

Closing (3 minutes)

Think about all the changes in your life while someone reads the following psalm.

God is our refuge and strength,
*   an ever-present help in trouble.*
Therefore we will not fear, though the
*   earth give way*
*   and the mountains fall into the heart of*
*   the sea,*
though its waters roar and foam
*   and the mountains quake with their surging.*
There is a river whose streams make glad the
*   city of God,*
*   the holy place where the Most High dwells.*
God is within her, she will not fall;
*   God will help her at break of day.*
Nations are in an uproar, kingdoms fall;
*   He lifts His voice, the earth melts.*
The LORD Almighty is with us;
*   the God of Jacob is our fortress.*
*   (Psalm 46:1–7)*

Change

Bible Reading

Keep your lives free from the love of money and be content with what you have, because God has said,

"Never will I leave you; never will I forsake you."

So we say with confidence,

"The Lord is my helper; I will not be afraid. What can man do to me?"

Remember your leaders, who spoke the word of God to you. Consider the outcome of their way of life and imitate their faith. Jesus Christ is the same yesterday and today and forever. *(Hebrews 13:5–8)*

Reflection

There are many skills that help us make our way through life. Perhaps most important is the skill of learning. With things changing so rapidly, flexibility and adaptation are necessary for survival. Real growth and development happens not only when learning new things but when unlearning old, comfortable behaviors. From our family of origin, we may bring many ways of acting that are not healthy. Because those actions are comfortable and familiar, it may feel unnatural to do anything else. It will take loving patience, clear determination, and God's help to change these familiar behaviors.

When making any changes, it is important to remember what your core values are. Your core values are what you believe regarding the purpose of life. For a Christian, Jesus Christ is the core value. Everything else is built upon Him. When you consider changes in yourself or in other family members, you can measure the worth of these changes by relating them to your core value. The discussion that follows will help you assess what your family considers to be its core values.

Family Time

Complete the following:
- What would you like to change about your family?
- What would you never want to change about your family?

Share your responses, but please refrain from commenting on one another's answers. Listen to everyone, then respond to the following:
- What things on the other lists surprised you?
- What did you agree with?
- What changes might you look to make in your family that would make things better for everyone?

Prayer Time

Dear Lord, create in me a new and right spirit. Change us where we need changing and uphold us in the things that will never change, such as Your love for us, forever. In Jesus' name. Amen.

funtastic family nights

7
Self-Esteem

Key Concept

The most important element in the well-being of a child is his or her self-concept or self-esteem. How a child sees himself or herself is at least partly the result of how parents see themselves. Parents build their child's self-esteem from the foundation of their own sense of well-being.

As Christians we base our self-esteem on the promise of God's unconditional love in Jesus Christ. As we receive this love from God through the Holy Spirit, we in turn give it to one another.

Objective

This event will help participants see their role as those who carry the gift of God's love. As evidence of that love, participants will practice giving and receiving affirmation, and they will explore ways to develop self-esteem.

Materials Checklist

☐ Poster board for each participant (approximately 16″ × 20″)

☐ Markers or crayons

☐ Name tags

☐ Copies of the Family Event Handout (one for each participant)

☐ Copies of the Take-home Page (one for each participating family)

As Participants Arrive—"This Is Me" Poster

Make your own poster (based on the instructions below) before the event and display it as an example for the posters you will ask participants to make. Next to it, post the following instructions. Read the instructions aloud to make sure everyone is aware of what to do with the poster.

Make a poster about yourself that uses only half of the poster board. Using drawings and images only, draw the following:

- Your name on top of one side
- Something you do well
- Your best time of day
- Something you are proud of

Remember to use only half the poster board. Invite everyone to make a name tag as well.

Opening Prayer

Dear heavenly Father of all fathers, You have loved us with an eternal love. Even when we were still sinners, You sent Jesus to rescue us. Help us remember and celebrate Your love for us. Empower us by Your Spirit to love one another in Jesus' name. Amen.

For Starters

Invite everyone to move about the group with their posters. Encourage everyone to find three people outside their own family and tell them about three things on their poster.

Handout Facilitation Suggestions

Ask the groups to send one person to gather the necessary materials from the supply table at the appropriate time. Remind them that even if smaller children may not respond to the questions, they will grow from being a part of the family discussion.

Give a copy of the handout to each person at the tables. Instruct them to respond to the questions and activities. Keep groups aware of the time and encourage them to move on to each portion of the handout.

Closing

The closing activity is on the Family Event Handout. Each family should do the closing activity in their family group. Then close with a group prayer or sing a hymn or song that is familiar to everyone.

Pass out the Take-home Page as families leave.

Self-Esteem

Activity—Pass the Poster (20 minutes)

Within your family group, pass your poster one person to the right. That person will draw a word or image on the empty portion of the poster board that describes what he or she loves about the person who made the poster. When everyone has finished, pass the posters to the right and repeat until everyone has his or her own poster again.

When everyone has his or her own poster, each person takes a turn interpreting what the words or symbols mean.

In the following passage, Jesus sums up all the commandments into two. Have someone read the text aloud.

> **"Love the Lord your God with all your heart and with all your soul and with all your mind and with all your strength." The second is this: "Love your neighbor as yourself." There is no commandment greater than these.**
> *(Mark 12: 30–31)*

Nine of the Ten Commandments begin with "You should *not* ..." But Jesus says the greatest commandments are about love—love for God and love for others.

Discuss as a family what positive actions you could do in your family to show love for God and for one another.

Closing—Love Bombardment (15 minutes)

One way we can love one another is to build one another's self-esteem through positive words of love. Take time to bombard each other with positive words.

Stand in a circle holding hands. The group will take turns bombarding each person with good words, compliments, affirmations. The person whose birthday is closest to today will go first. Ask that person to stand in the center of the circle as the others affirm him or her with statements of love and appreciation. Some examples include

♥ You are such a joy to me because ...

♥ What I love about you is ...

♥ You are a blessing to our family because ...

♥ It is fun to be with you because ...

When you are finished, be seated at your table and wait for everyone to finish.

Love for God with all your heart, soul, mind, and strength	Love for One Another as you love yourself

Self-Esteem

The Land of Buckets

Bible Reading

I have loved you with an everlasting love; I have drawn you with loving-kindness.
(Jeremiah 31:3)

Reflection

Read *The Land of Buckets* aloud, then discuss the meaning of this story.

- If love is the crystal water, what is the dipper?
- How full are the buckets at your work, school, church, or in your family?
- Why do you think the Backwaters could not keep the water taken from others?
- Why do you think the miserable Backwater had an empty bucket?

Discuss what it means to keep your buckets of love full in your family and in your home.

- What can you give to one another?
- What has God given to you?
- How do you share God's life-giving love with one another?

Prayer Time

Pray for and with each other after your discussion.

Once there was a land where all the people carried a bucket and a dipper. The bucket was for holding the crystal water the people needed for life. The dipper was for giving away the crystal water to others.

These people (we'll call them Backwaters) were positive people. They felt wonderful about themselves and others. They were positive and wonderful as long as their buckets were full. When their buckets ran low, their thoughts and feelings became low too. And if their buckets had no crystal water, they were miserable.

Now remember, the Backwaters had dippers too. The dippers were made so they could dip into their own bucket of crystal water and give it to another. Miraculously, when that happened their own water did not go down. In fact, to their surprise, the amount of water would actually increase.

Many Backwaters learned the secret of keeping a full bucket. Whenever they noticed someone with a low bucket, they would dip into their bucket and give the life-giving water away. And when they did, they felt even better about themselves. When a child was born into the Land of Buckets, everyone would gather to make sure the new Backwater, born with an empty bucket, received lots of crystal water. The life-giving crystal water flowed and everything was wonderful.

One dark day a miserable Backwater with an empty bucket decided that if he had no crystal water for giving, he would use his dipper for taking. And he did. When he dipped into the bucket of one especially happy friend, the friend felt the loss of water and went away sad. But for some mysterious reason, the taker was unable to put the water into his own bucket. The more desperate he became, the more he dipped into the buckets of others. When others felt their own buckets losing water, they would begin dipping too. All too soon the once wonderful land was full of people dipping into others' buckets for the crystal water. And for all the dipping, no one seemed to have enough water.

Yet there were a few who remembered the secret and kept their buckets full by using the dippers only for giving.

8
How Do You Measure Up?

Key Concept

Families are under pressure to measure up to society's standards. God's standard for us is very high. We know that Jesus is the only one who reached the mark of perfection. His perfect life and His forgiveness form the basis of our assessment of our family.

Bible Passages

1 Samuel 16
Micah 5:2–4
Galatians 5:22–23

Objective

Participants will explore society's standards and think through how we sometimes use those standards to assess one another. That kind of assessment always leads to a lessening of our sense of self-worth. This event will focus on God's priorities—values that give us a more effective value system. The event will help participants realize God's love for them is the foundation for healthy self-esteem.

Materials Checklist

☐ Measuring tape

☐ Name tags and markers

☐ Wall chart for measuring height

☐ Construction paper

☐ Scissors

☐ Glue

☐ Stapler

☐ Glitter

☐ Copies of the Family Event Handout (one for each participant)

☐ Copies of Take-home Page (one for each participating family)

As Participants Arrive—How Tall Are You?

Make a wall chart for measuring height. Ask each person to make a name tag and put his or her height on it to the nearest half inch. Have a measuring tape for infants so their name tags also can have their height.

For Starters

Invite everyone to make one long line of people. Begin with the tallest person and end with the shortest person. Then form a circle. Help the group recognize where the infants in arms would be. Ask everyone to think of one word to describe their day for use in the opening prayer.

Opening Prayer

The prayer will be a circle praise prayer from the tallest to the shortest. Begin the prayer:

> **Dear heavenly Father, we praise You today for everything. If our day was great, we thank You. If our day was less than great, still we thank You. Lord, we praise You for this day that was (each person takes a turn, then end with) Amen.**

Handout Facilitation Suggestions

Ask the groups to send one person to gather the necessary materials from the supply table at the appropriate time. Remind them that even if smaller children may not respond to the questions, they will grow from being a part of the family discussion.

Give a copy of the handout to each person at the tables. Instruct them to respond to the questions and activities. Keep groups aware of the time and encourage them to move on to each portion of the handout.

Closing

Choose eight people from the group to pantomime the Bible story of God choosing David. Ask an adult to be Samuel. Ask seven children to be David's brothers.

You can retell the story in your own words or read it from the Bible. Ask the children to pass by Samuel. As each child passes, Samuel listens as if hearing God's voice, then shakes his head no. Then go into the group and find a toddler, asking, "Who will God choose to be the next king of Israel?" Lead the young child by Samuel, who smiles and shakes his head yes. Samuel places a crown on the child and holds him up for all to see. Applaud for God's chosen one.

Sing a favorite hymn. Pass out the Take-home Page as families leave.

How Do You Measure Up?

Activity (10 minutes)

Identify as many ways as possible in which you are being measured. Join together to make one list for your family. Encourage everyone to offer suggestions.

How does your family measure up? Are you average? above average? below average? What would it be like if you were below average in every measurement?

generous

Activity—A Crown of the Heart (15 minutes)

What kinds of things did God see in David that cannot be measured? Talk together around the table and decide what quality of the heart best describes each person. Make a crown for each person with that quality written on the front. Use construction paper, scissors, markers, stapler, glue, and glitter to construct the crowns.

How Do You Measure Up?

Focus
(5 minutes)

The following is the story of how God chose David. Read it aloud and listen to what God thinks is important.

The LORD said to Samuel, "How long will you mourn for Saul, since I have rejected him as king over Israel? Fill your horn with oil and be on your way; I am sending you to Jesse of Bethlehem. I have chosen one of his sons to be king." ... But the LORD said to Samuel, "Do not consider his appearance or his height, for I have rejected him. The LORD does not look at the things man looks at. Man looks at the outward appearance, but the LORD looks at the heart."

Then Jesse called Abinadab and had him pass in front of Samuel. But Samuel said, "The LORD has not chosen this one either." Jesse then had Shammah pass by, but Samuel said, "Nor has the LORD chosen this one." Jesse had seven of his sons pass before Samuel, but Samuel said to him, "The LORD has not chosen these." So he asked Jesse, "Are these all the sons you have?"

"There is still the youngest," Jesse answered, "but he is tending the sheep."

Samuel said, "Send for him; we will not sit down until he arrives."

So he sent and had him brought in. He was ruddy, with a fine appearance and handsome features.

Then the LORD said, "Rise and anoint him; he is the one."

So Samuel took the horn of oil and anointed him in the presence of his brothers, and from that day on the Spirit of the Lord came upon David in power. *(1 Samuel 16:1, 7–13)*

Closing
(5 minutes)

Ask each family member to complete the following sentence:

My favorite thing about our family is ...

funtastic family nights

How Do You Measure Up?

Bible Reading

This Bible passage discusses the small town of Bethlehem. How was it great?

But you, Bethlehem Ephrathah,
though you are small among the clans
of Judah,
out of you will come for me
one who will be ruler over Israel,
whose origins are from of old,
from ancient times.
Therefore Israel will be abandoned
until the time when she who is in labor
gives birth
and the rest of his brothers return
to join the Israelites.
He will stand and shepherd his flock
in the strength of the LORD,
in the majesty of the name of the LORD
his God.
And they will live securely, for then his
greatness
will reach to the ends of the earth.
(Micah 5:2–4)

Reflection—
Self-Esteem

God's love for us is the foundation for healthy self-esteem. God has a very high opinion of people: He sent His Son to be a person. Whether you are a wife, husband, or child, your self-esteem is important for your family's well-being. Sometimes God's opinion of us gets overshadowed by the low opinion others have of themselves. Think about it: If someone says or does something to lower your sense of self-worth, they do it because of their own low self-esteem. People with a high sense of self-worth do not have to put others down. God did not send Jesus to put us in our place, but to exalt us, to lift us up to the highest levels of worth and value.

One necessary foundation for self-esteem, especially in the younger years, is respect and affirmation from others. Parents who understand this do not focus on their child's weaknesses, but on the child's worth and value. Self-esteem is at least partly the result of being respected and valued. Parents who know this manage to direct their children without stepping on their dignity and their self-esteem. First, parents need to remember how much God loves them, then they will be ready to support and nurture their children's opinion of self.

How Do You Measure Up?

Your Family's Score
Fruit of the Spirit

	low									high
love	1	2	3	4	5	6	7	8	9	10
joy	1	2	3	4	5	6	7	8	9	10
peace	1	2	3	4	5	6	7	8	9	10
patience	1	2	3	4	5	6	7	8	9	10
kindness	1	2	3	4	5	6	7	8	9	10
goodness	1	2	3	4	5	6	7	8	9	10
faithfulness	1	2	3	4	5	6	7	8	9	10
gentleness	1	2	3	4	5	6	7	8	9	10
self-control	1	2	3	4	5	6	7	8	9	10

Family Time—What Is Worth Measuring?

Read the Bible passage below, then rank your family concerning the fruit of the Spirit.

But the fruit of the Spirit is love, joy, peace, patience, kindness, goodness, faithfulness, gentleness and self-control. Against such things there is no law. *(Galatians 5:22–23)*

Discuss how the rankings given by members of the family reflect the strengths of your family. What areas still need attention? In what ways can you ask the Holy Spirit to demonstrate evidence of a particular fruit in you?

Prayer Time

Dear Jesus, we thank You for Your gift of love and forgiveness. Your love for us is unconditional. Your love was given to save us. Help us to love and forgive ourselves as we love and forgive others. We pray this in the name of the one who lived, died, and rose again, Christ Jesus our Lord. Amen.

9 Follow the Leader

Key Concept

Jesus has the power to transform our lives from an earthly focus to a focus on the eternal. We are better able to follow Jesus when we have role models after whom we can pattern our lives.

Bible Passage

Philippians 3:17–21

Objective

Participants will playfully consider the idea of following the lead of others and reflect on the truth that Jesus is the only one worthy of our imitation. Families will develop a greater appreciation for the idea of modeling behaviors for one another.

Materials Checklist

☐ Construction paper

☐ Name tags and markers

☐ Poster board

☐ Cookie cutters and play dough

☐ Copies of the Family Event Handout (one for each participant)

☐ Copies of the Take-home Page (one for each participating family)

As Participants Arrive—Give Me a Hand

As families arrive ask everyone to prepare a name tag. Then ask them to make a family "hands" poster. They are to trace their hands on construction paper, cut the hands out, then paste them on the poster board. They can write their family name at the top of the poster or in the center. Each family should display the poster on their table during the event.

Opening Prayer

You might ask a child to read the following prayer to begin the event.

> **Dear Jesus, thank You for choosing us and making us citizens of Your heavenly kingdom. Help us to learn together now and open our hearts and minds to You and to one another. Amen.**

For Starters

Invite everyone to play "Simon Peter Says." The rules are similar to "Simon Says," only the phrase is "Simon Peter Says." Those who do actions that aren't prefaced by "Simon Peter says" return to their seats. Below are some suggestions for the game. Add to the list as needed. Use a few practice rounds to make sure everyone understands the rules.

Simon Peter Says

Stand up.

Hop on one foot.

Wink at three people.

Shake hands with five people.

Hold hands with your family.

Shout alleluia.

Clap your hands three times.

Write your name in the air.

Raise your arms above your head and say "so big."

Do a high five with one other person.

Shout your name out loud.

Give someone a back rub.

Handout Facilitation Suggestions

Ask the groups to send one person to gather the necessary materials from the supply table at the appropriate time. Remind them that even if smaller children may not respond to the questions, they will grow from being a part of the family discussion.

Give a copy of the handout to each person at the tables. Instruct them to respond to the questions and activities. Keep groups aware of the time and encourage them to move on to each portion of the handout.

Closing

Close your event with a familiar "action song." Encourage children to teach everyone a song they have learned in Sunday school or vacation Bible school that includes actions. Make sure the children understand they are the "leaders" for the closing worship—leaders because they are teaching about Jesus.

Pass out the Take-home Page as families leave.

Follow the Leader

Activity—Follow the Leader (10 minutes)

It's time for a game of "Follow the Leader" with an interesting twist. You will need at least five people to play this game. If your family has four members or less, join another family and continue.

To play the game, everyone should imitate one leader at the table. The leader should make big motions with hands, arms, and head, changing from one motion to another. The first person to be "it" is the one whose birthday is closest to today. Ask the person who is "it" to cover his or her eyes while you choose the first leader.

Everyone begins to move, but gradually the group follows the appointed leader. The person who is "it" attempts to discover who the leader is. When the leader is discovered, that individual becomes "it." The first "it" chooses a new leader.

Play the game for 10 minutes, then return to individual family tables.

Focus—Who's the Leader? (10 minutes)

Ask someone at your table to read the following passage aloud. Think about the game you just played as you read and hear God's Word.

> **Join with others in following my example, brothers, and take note of those who live according to the pattern we gave you. For, as I have often told you before and now say again even with tears, many live as enemies of the cross of Christ. Their destiny is destruction, their god is their stomach, and their glory is in their shame. Their mind is on earthly things. But our citizenship is in heaven. And we eagerly await a Savior from there, the Lord Jesus Christ, who, by the power that enables Him to bring everything under His control, will transform our lowly bodies so that they will be like His glorious body. (Philippians 3:17–21)**

During the reading and discussion of the Bible passage, the children can use the cookie cutters and play dough to make different shapes. Use the following questions to discuss the passage.

Follow the Leader

❏ How does this passage remind you of the game?

❏ What insights do you have about the passage from your experience playing the game?

❏ Because your citizenship is in heaven, can you think of any ways that your family imitates the apostle Paul?

❏ How can children set a good example for their parents?

   Remind everyone that we can be like Jesus, using Him as our pattern (cookie cutter).

Closing (5 minutes)

   Ask one another to reflect on these questions:

• What does Paul mean when he writes "their god is their stomach"?

• What other "gods" do we worship?

   In this passage, Paul lifts up two groups with opposite ways of living: those who live as enemies of the cross of Christ and those who live as citizens of heaven. On our own, we can only be enemies of Christ. Our minds are naturally set "on earthly things." We know that it is the power of Jesus Christ that enables us to get our priorities straight. By His death and resurrection, Jesus Christ makes us citizens of heaven. Take time now to privately confess your "stomach god" and complete the following prayer:

> **I confess that my mind is often set on earthly things. Thank You, Jesus, for freeing me from the stomach god of _____. Amen.**

funtastic family nights

Follow the Leader

Bible Reading

Join with others in following my example, brothers, and take note of those who live according to the pattern we gave you. For, as I have often told you before and now say again even with tears, many live as enemies of the cross of Christ. Their destiny is destruction, their god is their stomach, and their glory is in their shame. Their mind is on earthly things. But our citizenship is in heaven. And we eagerly await a Savior from there, the Lord Jesus Christ, who, by the power that enables Him to bring everything under His control, will transform our lowly bodies so that they will be like His glorious body. *(Philippians 3:17–21)*

Reflection—Modeling

Consider the following statement from a 45-year-old father of three:

Well, I did it again. I just went into a long monolog, telling my daughter the virtues of being on time. It was an excellent speech, complete with introduction, four main points, and a summarized conclusion. I used colorful examples, dramatic inflection, and expressive descriptions. I wonder if I will remember those words the next time I'm late. I remember my father telling me about proper posture over and over again. He was a sloucher; so am I. Still, I can give a stirring lecture.

Everyone learns about life in some kind of family. Healthy or not, people tend to speak, act, and think according to the "rules" of their family of origin. It may be more comfortable to continue to behave in a hurtful, even unhealthy, way if that is the way our family system "worked." You already may know what your harmful patterns of behavior are.

Here are some things to consider when attempting to change hurtful ways from the past.

1. You are not alone or hopelessly trapped. You are loved and forgiven through Jesus. You are growing anew each day through the power of the Holy Spirit.

2. Those "old" ways are not something you learn; they are something you unlearn.

3. It took a childhood to learn your old patterns of behavior. It will take a long-term commitment to unlearn them. Life with Christ is a relationship, not a job description.

4. Decide what is most important and work on that. Make a plan and monitor your progress.

5. Pray for God to lead you, support you, and free you to be a new creature in Christ.

funtastic family nights

Follow the Leader

Family Time

Take out two sheets of paper. Title one "How I Want My Parent(s) to Be" and title the other "How I Want My Child(ren) to Be."

Parent(s) go first. List the things you want to see most in your children. Write them out so everyone can read them. Now help each child, one at a time, to write what he or she wants to see most in his or her parent(s). Younger children can participate by telling you what to write. It is important to write these items down—even the youngest children will remember which words are theirs.

The wonderful truth about human behavior is that if we want someone else to change, we have to change ourselves. That means the list the children made is really for them and the parents' list is really for the parents to follow. Jesus said, "First take the plank out of your own eye, and then you will see clearly to remove the speck from your brother's eye" (Matthew 7:5).

Prayer Time

Write a song about your family to the tune of "Are You Sleeping?" It could begin with, "We are fam'ly, we are fam'ly ..." Write it on a large sheet of paper so everyone can see it. Teach the words to younger children. Sing it together.

10 Feelings Are Blessings

Key Concept

Feelings are a wonderful gift from God. We can learn to accept and appreciate our feelings and the feelings of others. Expressing our feelings helps build relationships.

Bible Passages

Philippians 1:1–9
John 13:31–34

Objective

Participants will learn that all feelings are gifts from God. They will learn to recognize and identify the feelings of others. Participants also will learn that expressing both positive and negative feelings leads to closer and more authentic relationships.

Materials Checklist

☐ Mystery box (several boxes that can hold objects with a variety of textures). Find two or three boxes that are large enough for an adult to reach inside with his or her hand. Cut a hole in one side of each box. Cut the toes out of two or three athletic socks. Glue or staple one end of each sock around the opening on each box. Participants will stick their hands through the socks to reach inside the boxes and feel the "secret" items. Place interesting things inside the boxes (for example, a pine cone, a sponge, a potato, or a ball of aluminum foil).

☐ Name tags and markers

☐ 8½ × 11 paper

☐ Newsprint

☐ Several pictures that show human emotion (look in magazines or in your family photo albums)

☐ Copies of the Family Event Handout (one for each participant)

☐ Copies of the Take-home Page (one for each participating family)

As Participants Arrive—*Feel* with Your *Fingers; Feel* with Your *Heart*

As everyone arrives, ask them to prepare a name tag. Then invite each person to reach into the mystery boxes and describe what the object inside "feels" like.

At another location, invite everyone to examine the pictures that depict human emotion. Ask everyone to describe the feelings of those pictured.

Participants also should use a marker and an 8½″ × 11″ sheet of paper to draw a picture or write a word or short phrase that describes how they felt during most of the day.

Opening Prayer

Dear heavenly Father, we thank You for our emotions. Help us to see them as wonderful gifts of life and to use them to better understand one another. Send Your Holy Spirit so we can celebrate in sighs too deep for words. Amen.

For Starters

Bring everyone together at their family tables and say:

Welcome everyone! How are you feeling today? (Pause.) Perhaps a better question is: *What* are you feeling today? Today we are going to explore the truth that our emotions are a wonderful gift from God. We are going to practice sharing our feelings and listening for the feelings of others. We will see how listening for feelings and not judging them is a great way to communicate with one another.

Ask participants to hold in front of them the sheet of paper with the picture, word, or short phrase that describes their feelings as they walk around the room. As they meet someone with the same or similar feeling, participants should stop briefly and discuss why they have that feeling.

Handout Facilitation Suggestions

Ask the groups to send one person to gather the necessary materials from the supply table at the appropriate time. Remind them that even if smaller children may not respond to the questions, they will grow from being a part of the family discussion.

Give a copy of the handout to each person at the tables. Instruct them to respond to the questions and activities. Keep groups aware of the time and encourage them to move on to each portion of the handout.

Write "I feel *that* ..." on a chalkboard or a sheet of newsprint. Discuss how the word *that* changes the message from a feeling to a thought or opinion. For example:

I feel satisfied. (feeling)

I feel that things are going well. (thought or opinion)

Even negative feelings help us understand one another better. Invite everyone to practice describing their feelings and learning to accept the feelings of others.

Closing

Gather the group into a circle and ask for any comments or evaluations of the activities. Listen to the comments without defending or objecting to what is said. Close with the following blessing:

Hear the words of the apostle Paul to you this evening: "I thank my God every time I remember you. In all my prayers for all of you, I always pray with joy because of your partnership in the gospel from the first day until now, being confident of this, that He who began a good work in you will carry it on to completion until the day of Christ Jesus" (Philippians 1:3–6).

Pass out the Take-home Page as families leave.

Feelings Are Blessings

Focus (15 minutes)

Telling others how we think and feel is one way we communicate in our family. Both thinking and feeling are essential to constructive communication. In general, thinking ("head talk") leads to explanations while feeling ("heart talk") leads to understanding.

The following greeting from the apostle Paul has been divided into sections. Look at each section and discuss what Paul's feelings might have been.

God can testify how I long for all of you with the affection of Christ Jesus. *(Philippians 1:8)*

Feelings

_____
_____
_____

Paul and Timothy, servants of Christ Jesus, To all the saints in Christ Jesus at Philippi, together with the overseers and deacons: Grace and peace to you from God our Father and the Lord Jesus Christ. I thank my God every time I remember you. In all my prayers for all of you, I always pray with joy because of your partnership in the gospel from the first day until now. *(Philippians 1:1–5)*

Feelings

_____
_____
_____

It is right for me to feel this way about all of you, since I have you in my heart; for whether I am in chains or defending and confirming the gospel, all of you share in God's grace with me. *(Philippians 1:7)*

Feelings

_____
_____
_____

Being confident of this, that He who began a good work in you will carry it on to completion until the day of Christ Jesus. *(Philippians 1:6)*

Feelings

_____
_____
_____

And this is my prayer: that your love may abound more and more in knowledge and depth of insight. *(Philippians 1:9)*

Feelings

_____
_____
_____

☆

funtastic family nights

Feelings Are Blessings

Activity (15 minutes)

This is not only an exercise in expressing feelings, it is an opportunity to share with one another at a deeper level. Share your feelings about your family. Do not explain thoughts—simply share feelings. Leave out the word *that*. When you say, "I feel *that* ..." you are expressing a thought, not a feeling.

Complete the following sentence stems:

- When I am away from the family, I feel . . .
- When I fail at something, I feel . . .
- When we are together, I feel . . .
- When we argue, I feel . . .
- Right now I am feeling . . .

Each person may take a turn sharing answers to the first statement, then the second, and so on until you finish or time is up. Do not make any judgments about others' feelings, *just listen* without interrupting.

Closing (5 minutes)

Hold hands and finish the following prayer stem:

I thank You, Jesus, for ...

Say together the following Bible verse:

A new command I give you: Love one another. As I have loved you, so you must love one another. *(John 13:34)*

funtastic family nights

Feelings Are Blessings

Reflection

Telling others what you think is the *prose* of communication; sharing what your heart is feeling is the *poetry*. Unfortunately, most of us communicate in "think" statements. We are asked for facts: "Where did you put the car keys?" or "What time will you be home?" and "Do you think you can come straight home from school?" Certainly, we do need to communicate the facts and our thoughts.

But families need to share more than thoughts. They need to express their feelings as well. Telling someone how we feel is the way we develop a stronger sense of closeness.

Your feelings belong to you. No one can make you feel anything. Owning your feelings is the first step in communicating them. Effective family communication occurs when individuals (especially parents) take responsibility for their thoughts, feelings, and behavior—that is, when they own what they do. When you own your thoughts and feelings, the other person knows what you are experiencing and can respond more authentically to you.

Bible Reading

For you know that it was not with perishable things such as silver or gold that you were redeemed from the empty way of life handed down to you from your forefathers, but with the precious blood of Christ, a lamb without blemish or defect. He was chosen before the creation of the world, but was revealed in these last times for your sake. Through Him you believe in God, who raised Him from the dead and glorified Him, and so your faith and hope are in God.

Now that you have purified yourselves by obeying the truth so that you have sincere love for your brothers, love one another deeply, from the heart. For you have been born again, not of perishable seed, but of imperishable, through the living and enduring word of God. *(1 Peter 1:18–23)*

funtastic family nights

Feelings Are Blessings

Family Time—Structured Time with the Photo Album

Schedule a time for your family to be together and share feelings. Get out the family photo album, baby books, or videos. Ask each member to choose three special pictures or video moments. Each person takes a turn and shares one selection and how he or she feels about it. Focus on the feelings and do not interrupt the sharing. Go around the circle three times. Then respond to the question, "What are you feeling right now?"

Closing

Sing a favorite childhood hymn or song or say a childhood prayer.

11

I'm Angry

Key Concept

Anger is one of the first emotions human beings experience and the last one we learn to manage effectively. It is possible to manage our anger. The key is love—love from God and love for one another. The power of God's love can empower our commitment to keep anger from turning into hateful actions.

Bible Passage

Ephesians 4:25–30

Objective

Participants will consider the destructive effects of unmanaged anger in the family. By looking at anger from a biblical perspective, they will give examples of how to handle anger in themselves and others.

Materials Checklist

- ☐ Video camera and a large playback monitor or television
- ☐ Name tags and markers
- ☐ 8½″ × 11″
- ☐ Toy blocks (a set for each family)
- ☐ Copies of the Family Event Handout (one for each participant)
- ☐ Copies of the Take-home Page (one for each participating family)

As Participants Arrive— Mug Shots

Have instructions written on a large sheet of poster board or on newsprint as follows:

Please Check In:

Make a name tag.

Have a mug shot made of yourself.

Find your table and make yourself at home.

Invite everyone to check in at the mug shot booth. Each person stands in front of the video camera and says, "Hi, my name is _____, and this is my angry face." Be sure to use a camera with a close-up zoom lens and take only short clips of each person.

Opening Prayer

Dear Lord, we know that feelings come and go. We can do little about them. Yet how we think and behave as a result of our feelings is our responsibility. Lord, live in our hearts and help us to behave in the way You would show us. Help us to deal with our anger in ways that promote love and strong relationships in our families. In Jesus' name. Amen.

For Starters

Show the video of angry faces. You will need to have a playback monitor that is adequate to the size of your group.

Handout Facilitation Suggestions

Ask the groups to send one person to gather the necessary materials from the supply table at the appropriate time. Remind them that even if smaller children may not respond to the questions, they will grow from being a part of the family discussion.

Give a copy of the handout to each person at the tables. Instruct them to respond to the questions and activities. Keep groups aware of the time and encourage them to move on to each portion of the handout.

Closing

Form a large circle. Ask everyone to turn and face the walls. Read the following:

Do not grieve the Holy Spirit of God, with whom you were sealed for the day of redemption. *(Pause.)* Get rid of all bitterness, rage and anger, brawling and slander, along with every form of malice, *(pause)* or of any kind of impurity, or of greed, because these are improper for God's holy people. *(Pause.)* Nor should there be obscenity, foolish talk or coarse joking. *(Pause.)* Have nothing to do with the fruitless deeds of darkness. *(Ephesians 4:30–31; 5:3–4; 11)*

Ask everyone to turn around and look at one another. Read the following.

For once you were darkness, but now you are light in the Lord. Live as children of light *(pause)* (for the fruit of the light consists in all goodness, righteousness, and truth) *(pause)* and find out what pleases the Lord. *(Pause.)* Be imitators of God, therefore, as dearly loved children and live a life of love, just as Christ loved us and gave Himself up for us as a fragrant offering and sacrifice to God. *(Pause.)* Be kind and compassionate to one another, forgiving each other, just as in Christ God forgave you. Amen. *(Ephesians 5:8–10; 5:1–2; 4:32)*

Dismiss the group with hugs and affirmations. Pass out the Take-home Page as families leave.

I'm Angry

Focus (5 minutes)

Ask someone to read the following aloud to the family.

During this time together, we are going to talk about one aspect of anger in family relationships. Like toy blocks stacked on top of each other, one block can cause the entire tower to fall—negative feelings, even small ones, can build up to the breaking point. If you don't deal with the little problems, the feelings can accumulate and become *anger*.

Activity—Building a Block Tower (10 minutes)

From the supply of building blocks, each person should take a block, tell one thing that makes him or her angry, and put the block in place, one on top of another.

If the tower falls, start over. If it doesn't fall, keep going until it does. Discuss how your family is like the block tower.

Reflection (10 minutes)

Identify a recent time when your family was living through an angry time. After you have identified the incident, ask someone to read the following passage aloud to the family.

Therefore each of you must put off falsehood and speak truthfully to his neighbor, for we are all members of one body. "In your anger do not sin": Do not let the sun go down while you are still angry, and do not give the devil a foothold. He who has been stealing must steal no longer, but must work, doing something useful with his own hands, that he may have something to share with those in need.

Do not let any unwholesome talk come out of your mouths, but only what is helpful for building others up according to their needs, that it may benefit those who listen. And do not grieve the Holy Spirit of God, with whom you were sealed for the day of redemption. *(Ephesians 4:25–30)*

Notice the passage did not say, "Don't be angry." Having angry feelings is not a sin. Doing angry things is wrong. Look at this passage again and think about the last time your family was angry. Respond to the following:

How do you think you might "speak truthfully" without being angry and without making someone else angry too?

Closing

Complete the following sentence, then have each person share:

Please forgive me for when I was angry and _____.

Close with a prayer for forgiveness.

I'm Angry

Reflection

If someone pinches you, you feel some discomfort. A "pinch" is what John J. Sherwood and John C. Glidewell have used to describe the feeling you get when someone does something that irritates you ("A Model for Couples: How to Grow Together" *Journal for Small Group Behavior,* 1977). Actions that pinch may not be obvious actions against you, but they are things that annoy—that pinch— and they can lead to frustration and exasperation.

If the "pinch" is not confronted and other pinches are added, it becomes a "crunch." A "crunch" can cause anger expressed in angry words and bitter feelings. As people grow closer to each other, the probability of conflict increases. In fact, it is not possible to have a relationship without some confrontation and conflict. Conflict can put an end to the relationship, or it can be a great opportunity to grow even closer together.

The Three Step

Here is a three-step approach for dealing constructively with pinches in the family:

Step ❶: Announce, "I am angry." When you are angry—and you do know when—make a clear announcement to everyone around you. This gives people the opportunity to stay clear of you for a while and gives you time to calm down.

Step ❷: Promise, "I will not act out my anger on anyone I care about." Immediately after you announce that you are angry, promise that you will not permit your anger to get out of control and that you will not direct it toward anyone at any time.

Step ❸: Schedule, "We will talk about this." It is essential that you schedule a specific time to talk about what made you angry.

After you can think clearly about the triggering event, you can discuss, learn, and grow closer because of it. If you skip this step, the problem and the anger will likely return. If you find that you become angry again during the discussion, go back to step 1.

Bible Reading

Therefore each of you must put off falsehood and speak truthfully to his neighbor, for we are all members of one body. "In your anger do not sin": Do not let the sun go down while you are still angry, and do not give the devil a foothold. He who has been stealing must steal no longer, but must work, doing something useful with his own hands, that he may have something to share with those in need.

Do not let any unwholesome talk come out of your mouths, but only what is helpful for building others up according to their needs, that it may benefit those who listen. And do not grieve the Holy Spirit of God, with whom you were sealed for the day of redemption. *(Ephesians 4:25–30)*

Family Time

Gather together, light some candles, and/or play soft music. Parent(s) read the Bible passage above. Then tell your children that you would like to talk about not giving the devil "a foothold" in your family.

Tell a story about your childhood: "When I was growing up, my parents handled their anger by … . It made me feel … . In our family I would like … . What do you think?"

12 Helpful Feedback

Key Concept

Helpful feedback in the family is important because it provides information that helps others decide whether their behaviors are appropriate. Positive feedback is information that reinforces behaviors we wish to encourage. There are also times when we need to correct and give negative feedback. But negative feedback in itself is not enough. The Bible says, "If You, O LORD, kept a record of sins, O Lord, who could stand? But with You there is forgiveness; therefore You are feared" (Psalm 130:3–4). God forgives all the mistakes we make against Him. Certainly we also should seek God's power to forgive each other.

Bible Passages

Galatians 6:1–5
Psalm 130:3–4

Objective

Participants will have the opportunity to practice giving and receiving feedback as a way to increase the quality of their relationships. They will see that the Bible intends for followers of Jesus to give one another feedback to help them in their spiritual growth.

Materials Checklist

☐ One-page handout as described in next section (one for each participant)

☐ Name tags and markers

☐ Large teaching model of the Johari Window

☐ Pencils

☐ Copies of the Family Event Handout (one for each participant)

☐ Copies of the Take-home Page (one for each participating family)

As Participants Arrive

Prepare a handout for each person with the following:

The Johari Window

The Johari Window	**SELF**	
	Things I Know	Things I Don't Know
FAMILY Things They Know about Me	Arena	Blind Spot
Things They Don't Know about Me	Facade	Unknown

The Window of Self-Awareness

Things I Know and You Know Too:

Things I Know and You Do Not Know:

Things You Know about Me and I Do Not Know:

Ask everyone to prepare a name tag. Then encourage everyone to fill in and discuss the sheet with at least five others.

Opening Prayer

Ask a child to lead the group in prayer.

For Starters—The Johari Window

Teach the communication model known as the Johari Window. You can read the text below and point to the appropriate portions of the model redrawn on newsprint. It would be more effective if you told participants about the model from your own understanding of the text below.

This window is a communication and feedback model designed to depict how we give and receive information about ourselves and others. The model is a four-paned window. Two columns represent the *self;* the first contains "things I know about myself," and the second contains "things I do not know about myself." The rows represent the *family*—the first row being "things they know about me" and the second being "things they do not know about me."

The Arena contains information that I know about myself and about which the family knows. The Arena increases in size as the level of individual to family trust and communication increases.

The Blind Spot is the information known about me by others but which I do not know about myself. This information may be in the form of body language, habits, tone of voice, style, etc. It can be amazing to learn how many items appear in this area. For people with large Blind Spots, learning to solicit feedback can be useful and enlightening.

The Facade is the area of information that I know about myself but which I withhold from others. This information may include feelings, prejudices, and past history. People have var-

ious motives for keeping secrets. Some, for example, may fear rejection or ridicule.

The Unknown contains things that neither I nor others know about me. Some of this material may be so far below the surface that I may never become aware of it. This information may include childhood memories, unrealized potential, and so on. Because knowing oneself completely is extremely unlikely, the Unknown in the Johari Window model is extended so part of it always remains unknown.

The boundaries of the panes are flexible. This means the individual can enlarge or reduce a column or row by increasing or decreasing the amount of feedback one gives and receives. One of the purposes of this model is to help people reduce the Blind Spot, to develop a receptive attitude, and to encourage others in the family to give feedback.

The goal of learning to give and solicit feedback is to move information from the Blind Spot and the Facade into the Arena. Through this process, new information also can move from the Unknown into the Arena. This movement is frequently called insight or inspiration. The Johari Window model gives people a framework through which they can practice giving and receiving feedback. The overall goal is that everyone will learn to be more accepting of themselves and others.

Handout Facilitation Suggestions

Ask the groups to send one person to gather the necessary materials from the supply table at the appropriate time. Remind them that even if smaller children may not respond to the questions, they will grow from being a part of the family discussion.

Give a copy of the handout to each person at the tables. Instruct them to respond to the questions and activities. Keep groups aware of the time and encourage them to move on to each portion of the handout.

Closing

Sing "What a Friend We Have in Jesus." Pass out the Take-home Page as families leave.

Helpful Feedback

Responsible and Trustworthy						Not Responsible or Trustworthy
Always home on time	1	2	3	4	5	Never come home on time
Do all the chores	1	2	3	4	5	Seldom do chores
Do very best in school	1	2	3	4	5	Need to be reminded to study
Make family aware of plans	1	2	3	4	5	Make plans but don't tell others
Choose good friends	1	2	3	4	5	Have friends who get in trouble
Have never used drugs	1	2	3	4	5	Use drugs (includes tobacco)
Have a safe driving record	1	2	3	4	5	High-risk driver
Can trust completely	1	2	3	4	5	Can't trust at all
Total						

Focus (10 minutes)

Read this passage aloud.

Brothers, if someone is caught in a sin, you who are spiritual should restore him gently. But watch yourself, or you also may be tempted. Carry each other's burdens, and in this way you will fulfill the law of Christ. If anyone thinks he is something when he is nothing, he deceives himself. Each one should test his own actions. Then he can take pride in himself, without comparing himself to somebody else, for each one should carry his own load. (Galatians 6:1–5)

Family members are most aware of one another's transgressions (wrongdoings). How does this passage suggest you should manage one another's wrongdoings?

Activity (20 minutes)

The above table provides a discussion of responsibility and trust.

Parent(s): How do you rate your children? (circle the number, then add for a total)

Children: How do you rate yourself? (circle the number, then add for a total)

Compare your scores. Lower scores indicate greater responsibility. Which categories had the greatest difference? Discuss the areas of greatest concern. Remember to give everyone an opportunity to share and to give feedback "gently."

Closing (5 minutes)

Take time to complete the following prayer stem. Then take turns saying the prayer together.

Dear Jesus, I confess that I am not always responsible to the family, especially in the area of _____. Forgive me and give me the power of Your love to begin a new life with the support of my family. (The last person says amen.)

funtastic family nights

Helpful Feedback

Bible Reading

Brothers, if someone is caught in a sin, you who are spiritual should restore him gently. But watch yourself, or you also may be tempted. Carry each other's burdens, and in this way you will fulfill the law of Christ. If anyone thinks he is something when he is nothing, he deceives himself. Each one should test his own actions. Then he can take pride in himself, without comparing himself to somebody else, for each one should carry his own load. *(Galatians 6:1–5)*

Family Time

Schedule a time for giving and receiving feedback. Read and discuss the above "tips" for feedback. Each person should choose one person and one issue to give feedback about. Choose issues that are not heavily charged with emotion.

Prayer Time

The Bible says, "If You, O LORD, kept a record of sins, O Lord, who could stand? But with You there is forgiveness; therefore You are feared" (Psalm 130:3–4).

If our heavenly Father forgives all the mistakes we make against Him, should we not also forgive one another?

Take turns going around the family circle, asking one another for forgiveness. When someone asks forgiveness, the response is "Because of Jesus Christ, I forgive you." It is so simple, yet so powerful.

Reflection

Helpful feedback in the family is important because it is information that helps others decide whether their behaviors are appropriate. Positive feedback is information that reinforces behaviors. Positive feedback seeks to catch each other doing something right. There are times when we need to correct and give negative feedback. We should see that as information that discourages behaviors by communicating that the actions were hurtful or did not have the intended effect.

When you give feedback, follow these tips for effective feedback:

- Be sure that your intention is to be helpful.
- If the recipient has not asked for feedback, check whether he or she is open to it.
- Deal only with behavior that can be changed.
- Deal with specific behavior, not generalities.
- Describe the behavior; do not evaluate it.
- Let the recipient know the impact that the behavior has on you.
- Use an "I statement" to accept responsibility for your own perceptions and emotions. ("I am fearful when you …" "I get angry when you …")
- Check to make sure that the recipient understood your message in the way you intended.
- Encourage the recipient to check the feedback with other people.

When someone receives feedback, especially parents from children, the recipient might consider these tips:

- When you ask for feedback, be specific in describing the behavior about which you want the feedback.
- Try not to act defensively or explain away the behavior at issue.
- Say, "Thank you."
- Think about the importance of someone giving you this gift. Even if it makes you feel defensive, it is a good and helpful gift.
- Summarize your understanding of the feedback.
- Share your thoughts and feelings about the feedback.

13
Care for One Another

Key Concept

When God made us, He placed us in community. God's people together are a sign of God's grace. As family members support and care for one another, they give witness to their head, Jesus Christ. When Jesus is the head of the family, all are servants to one another.

Bible Passage

1 Corinthians 12:20–27

Objective

Participants will consider their love and care for each other. They will reflect upon God's model for a caring community. They will affirm their love for one another in prayers and words of support.

Materials Checklist

☐ Magazines

☐ Poster board or construction paper (one per family)

☐ Name tags and markers

☐ Tape

☐ Glue

☐ Scissors

☐ Copies of the Family Event Handout (one for each participant)

☐ Copies of the Take-home Page (one for each participating family)

As Participants Arrive—Body Collage and Name Tag

Invite each family to make a collage of a whole body. Cut body parts from magazines and glue them onto a sheet of poster board or construction paper to make a collage of one body with many parts. Each family should make its own collage.

Make a name tag. Cut a body part from a magazine and glue it to your name tag. What part of the body best describes you in your family? For instance, you might choose a foot because you are always on the go.

For Starters

Invite participants to walk around the room and find three other people, not from their own family, to tell about their name tag.

Announce that the activities for this event focus on care for one another in the family.

Now you are the body of Christ, and each one of you is a part of it. *(1 Corinthians 12:27)*

Handout Facilitation Suggestions

Ask the groups to send one person to gather the necessary materials from the supply table at the appropriate time. Remind them that even if smaller children may not respond to the questions, they will grow from being a part of the family discussion.

Give a copy of the handout to each person at the tables. Instruct them to respond to the questions and activities. Keep groups aware of the time and encourage them to move on to each portion of the handout.

Closing

Sing "Jesus Loves Me, This I Know." Pass out the Take-home Page as families leave.

Care for One Another

Activity—How We See Our Family (15 minutes)

Answer any three of the following questions, then go around the family circle and share the responses. Give everyone a chance to share all their answers before you discuss them.

- What is the one most important thing for your family?

- What is a fun thing your family does together?

- When is one time everyone in your family is together?

- If you could change one thing about your family, what would it be?

- What is the one thing you like best about your family?

- How do you know the people in your family care about you?

Focus (10 minutes)

Ask someone to read the following passage aloud. As you listen, think about, then discuss how this passage applies to your family.

As it is, there are many parts, but one body. The eye cannot say to the hand, "I don't need you!" On the contrary, those parts of the body that seem to be weaker are indispensable, and the parts that we think are less honorable we treat with special honor. And the parts that are unpresentable are treated with special modesty, while our presentable parts need no special treatment. But God has combined the members of the body and has given greater honor to the parts that lacked it, so that there should be no division in the body, but that its parts should have equal concern for each other. If one part suffers, every part suffers with it; if one part is honored, every part rejoices with it.

Now you are the body of Christ, and each one of you is a part of it. *(1 Corinthians 12:20–27)*

Closing

Complete the following sentence and prayer for each member of your family:

> **I think I know what you are hoping for today. And my prayer for you is …**

Begin with one member of the family. Ask all the others to say their prayers for them. Then move to the next person and so on until everyone has been prayed for.

funtastic family nights

Care for One Another

Bible Reading

As it is, there are many parts, but one body. The eye cannot say to the hand, "I don't need you!" On the contrary, those parts of the body that seem to be weaker are indispensable, and the parts that we think are less honorable we treat with special honor. And the parts that are unpresentable are treated with special modesty, while our presentable parts need no special treatment. But God has combined the members of the body and has given greater honor to the parts that lacked it, so that there should be no division in the body, but that its parts should have equal concern for each other. If one part suffers, every part suffers with it; if one part is honored, every part rejoices with it.

Now you are the body of Christ, and each one of you is a part of it. *(1 Corinthians 12:20–27)*

Reflection

A hug is an important form of family communication. A hug is an action that says *love* more clearly than any words. A caring hug is always nonsexual. It is hard to harm or blame someone with a hug. With a hug, I say, "You are special, and I accept your feelings. You mean a lot to me. You are worthwhile."

Families can have a group hug that says we are all in this together. Hugs communicate a feeling of security. To a small child, a hug is a message that all is well. A teenager will get the same warm feeling—all is well. Hugs can say I trust you. A hug says I am happy when you are happy.

Give each other a hug and talk about what that action means to you. Plan to give a hug to at least one person every day during the coming week.

Family Time

Talk about the things that you are thinking and praying for. Share them with one another.

What I want for me ...

Then share what concerns you have for each family member.

What I want for you ...

Prayer Time

Take some time for everyone to think of a completion to the following prayer, then go around the room, lifting up the thoughts in prayer.

Dear Lord, I ask that You would bless our family with ...

14
I've Got a Secret

Key Concept

Too much and too little openness can be harmful in families. Closed communications can be just as dysfunctional as completely open expressions. Honesty and appropriate openness can work to build the family. Secrets in the family can be harmful. As those who have been redeemed in Christ, we cherish "speaking the truth in love." Speaking and acting on the truth can contribute to healthy family relationships.

Bible Passages

Luke 12:1–3
Romans 8:24–27
Ephesians 4:14–16

Objective

Participants will understand the importance of openness and honesty in a growing and healthy family. At the same time they will develop a sensitivity to inappropriate openness that can become destructive. Through these activities, families will have a chance to practice open communication and see the benefit that such openness in love can have.

Materials Checklist

☐ Two or three mystery boxes (see session 10)

☐ Name tags and markers

☐ Blindfolds (optional)

☐ Pencils

☐ Copies of the Family Event Handout (one for each participant)

☐ Copies of the Take-home Page (one for each participating family)

As Participants Arrive

Ask everyone to prepare a name tag. Place two or three mystery boxes on a table in the center of your room. (See session 10 for directions to make a mystery box.) Place four things in each box and invite participants to feel and discover what the items are.

Suggestions for the "mystery" items include pine cone, golf ball, ball of yarn, paperweight, keys, tape measure, apple, or calculator.

Opening Prayer—Confession and Absolution

People: Holy and gracious God, I confess that I have sinned against You this day. Some of my sins I know—the thoughts and words and deeds of which I am ashamed—but some are known only to You. In the name of Jesus Christ, I ask forgiveness. Deliver and restore me that I may rest in peace.

Leader: By the mercy of God we are redeemed by Jesus Christ, and in Him we are forgiven. We rest now in His peace and rise in the morning to serve Him (*LW*, page 264).

For Starters—I've Got a Secret

Play a game of "I've Got a Secret" with a participant who has an interesting past or a unique skill. You might ask your pastor for assistance in choosing someone. Don't overlook a young person who has a special talent. You may wish to line up several special guests.

Choose a panel of eight people from the audience. The panel should include youth and adults from different families. Each panel member takes a turn asking questions, one at a time. The guest answers only yes or no. The guest gets a point for every no answer.

For a variation you might blindfold the panel members and ask them to guess who the special guest is. The guest should be someone everyone would know. The special guest may have to disguise his or her voice.

Handout Facilitation Suggestions

Ask the groups to send one person to gather the necessary materials from the supply table at the appropriate time. Remind them that even if smaller children may not respond to the questions, they will grow from being a part of the family discussion.

Give a copy of the handout to each person at the tables. Instruct them to respond to the questions and activities. Keep groups aware of the time and encourage them to move on to each portion of the handout.

Closing

Form circles of 15 people and hold hands. Give each circle a button and tell them to place the youngest person in the middle of the circle and play "Button, Button Who Has the Button?" Remember, the people in the circle pass the button around the circle in one direction. The person who is "it" points to whoever he or she thinks has the button until someone is caught with the it. Then that person becomes "it."

Allow groups to play this game for several rounds. Then ask everyone to join hands as you read the following text:

> **Then we will no longer be infants, tossed back and forth by the waves, and blown here and there by every wind of teaching and by the cunning and craftiness of men in their deceitful scheming. Instead, speaking the truth in love, we will in all things grow up into Him who is the Head, that is, Christ. From Him the whole body, joined and held together by every supporting ligament, grows and builds itself up in love, as each part does its work. (Ephesians 4:14–16)**

Pass out the Take-home Page as families leave.

I've Got a Secret

Activity—Three Truths and a Lie (15 minutes)

This is a fun and challenging game for families to play. Each person writes four things about themselves—three are little known truths; one of the items is not true. The object of the game is to fool the others into guessing that one of the truths is the lie.

Some examples might include ⟶

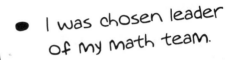

- I was chosen leader of my math team.
- I used to have a crush on my third-grade teacher.
- I had the lowest score on a history test.
- _____

Focus (15 minutes)

Ask someone in your family to read the following Bible passage. Then read and discuss the questions below it.

> **Meanwhile, when a crowd of many thousands had gathered, so that they trampled on one another, Jesus began to speak first to His disciples, "Be on your guard against the yeast of the Pharisees, which is hypocrisy. There is nothing concealed that will not be disclosed, or hidden that will not be made known. What you have said in the dark will be heard in the daylight, and what you have whispered in the ear in the inner rooms will be proclaimed from the roof.** (Luke 12:1–3)

- Why would you not tell your family everything?
- Are there some things you have determined never to tell anyone?
- What about things that have to do with the health and well-being of individuals?
- Why would you consider keeping anything a secret in the family?
- What are the risks of secrecy?

God knows all things and perhaps it is best that only He knows. Yet some things are too important to hide from one another. What might they be?

Closing (5 minutes)

There is a relationship even closer than our family's. Read the following passage and consider how close the Holy Spirit is to us, even as we speak.

> **For in this hope we were saved. But hope that is seen is no hope at all. Who hopes for what he already has? But if we hope for what we do not yet have, we wait for it patiently.**
>
> **In the same way, the Spirit helps us in our weakness. We do not know what we ought to pray for, but the Spirit Himself intercedes for us with groans that words cannot express. And He who searches our hearts knows the mind of the Spirit, because the Spirit intercedes for the saints in accordance with God's will.** (Romans 8:24–27)

I've Got a Secret

Bible Reading

Then we will no longer be infants, tossed back and forth by the waves, and blown here and there by every wind of teaching and by the cunning and craftiness of men in their deceitful scheming. Instead, speaking the truth in love, we will in all things grow up into Him who is the Head, that is, Christ. From Him the whole body, joined and held together by every supporting ligament, grows and builds itself up in love, as each part does its work. *(Ephesians 4:14–16)*

Reflection

Too much and too little openness can be harmful in families. Closed communications can be just as dysfunctional as completely open expressions. Honesty and openness can work to build the family. Secrets in the family can be harmful. As those who have been redeemed in Christ, we cherish "speaking the truth in love." A family that can tolerate honest interchange of thoughts and feelings has developed a trusting relationship and an ability to be sensitive to one another. As people in such families interact, they are free to give, receive, and elicit feedback about the effects of their own and others' behavior.

Family Time—Making a Family Promise

Set aside time for a special family discussion. Choose a time when you are not dealing with mistrust or allegations of lying. Use the time to focus on the positive.

Have a discussion regarding the following thoughts. Record all the ideas listed.

* We are the _____ family.
* We believe in _____.
* What is important to us is _____.
* So we will always _____.

Then speak this promise to one another:

We promise to each other and to Jesus that this is how we would like to be with one another. When anyone is unable or unwilling to keep this promise, we will remind them, forgive them, and expect

Destructive openness can result from "telling it like it is." Confrontational honesty can be insensitive or hostile. If the effect of open self-disclosure is to make another person defensive or anxious, the exchange will very likely be destructive. If the open communication is markedly judgmental of others, the chance that it will be harmful is increased. For example, a wife asks her husband about her haircut. Even though he may be unhappy with the cut, total openness would not be effective communication. On the other hand, he need not be "dishonest." He simply might describe the cut in words that do not convey a judgment. In that way he can defuse the situation and seek to deal with the haircut at a more appropriate time.

Openness with integrity and honesty promotes growth in a family and fosters effective communication. Being effectively open implies a responsibility to check out other family members carefully, being alert to cues that indicate boundaries.

Prayer Time
Using the promise you have written, write a song to the melody of "Mary Had a Little Lamb" or "Row, Row, Row Your Boat."

funtastic family nights

It Takes More than Love

15

Key Concept

Love is both a noun and a verb. God's love is both something that He is and something He does for us in an action of rescue and deliverance. Love in a family is demonstrated in actions of commitment and responsibility toward one another. Families need to take an honest look at how they are acting in love for one another.

Bible Passage

1 Peter 4:8–10

Objective

Participants will look honestly at behaviors that express their love and their responsibilities toward one another. Participants will celebrate the love they receive from God and the love they share with one another. They also will be encouraged to consider listening as an act of love.

Materials Checklist

☐ Make a large poster board sign that says "LOVE IS ..."

☐ Red construction paper

☐ Masking tape

☐ Name tags and markers

☐ Copies of the Family Event Handout (one for each participant)

☐ Copies of the Take-home Page (one for each participating family)

As Participants Arrive— Love Is ...

Ask participants to prepare a name tag. Then invite them to tear out or cut out hearts from red construction paper. On the hearts they should write or draw what love is or means to them.

Opening Prayer

Invite a participant to read 1 Corinthians 13.

For Starters

Invite volunteers to tape their hearts on the wall next to the sign. As they do so, invite them to tell what love is or means to them.

Handout Facilitation Suggestions

Ask the groups to send one person to gather the necessary materials from the supply table at the appropriate time. Remind them that even if smaller children may not respond to the questions, they will grow from being a part of the family discussion.

Give a copy of the handout to each person at the tables. Instruct them to respond to the questions and activities. Keep groups aware of the time and encourage them to move on to each portion of the handout.

Closing

Ask the families to think about the evening. How well did you listen to one another? Did you interrupt one another while speaking? State that listening is said to be the language of love. It is not a coincidence that our heavenly Father listens to us quietly, patiently, and knowingly, then acts in our behalf with grace and power.

Close with this prayer:

Thank You, God, for being there to listen ... listen ... listen ... . Amen.

Pass out the Take-home Page as families leave.

It Takes More than Love

Focus (5 minutes)

Read the following passage aloud together. The text and the questions that follow will help you discuss what constant love for one another might feel like in your family.

> **Above all, love each other deeply, because love covers over a multitude of sins. Offer hospitality to one another without grumbling. Each one should use whatever gift he has received to serve others, faithfully administering God's grace in its various forms.** *(1 Peter 4:8–10)*

Activity (20 minutes)

Dr. Nick Stennett of the University of Nebraska identified qualities of strong families. Read the descriptions to the right. Choose the two your family does well. Write S for strength on the line provided. Then choose the two that need more work. Write a C for challenge on the line.

Go around the table and ask each person to share his or her choices and why the choice was made. Do not interrupt. Use the grid below to celebrate your strengths and discover your challenges.

Closing (5 minutes)

Complete the prayer stems, then pray together.

> **Thank You, Jesus, for giving us the family strength of _____. Send Your Holy Spirit to help us grow in the challenge of _____. Amen.**

① **Appreciation** ____
- building up others in the family
- making others feel good about themselves
- express joy because of others

② **Spending Time Together** ____
- enjoy being together
- good quality time
- just doing things such as working, eating, or recreation

③ **Good Communication Patterns** ____
- when you spend time together, there is listening and talking
- you argue, but in an open way about your differences
- you talk about how you feel inside

④ **Commitment to Family** ____
- support each other in family
- promote each other's happiness and welfare
- keep family a priority, even if life is busy

⑤ **High Degree of Religious Orientation** ____
- go to church together
- participate in church activities together
- live a spiritually centered life at home

⑥ **Deals with Crisis in a Positive Way** ____
- you do have crises, but you deal with them constructively
- you stick together
- you support each other and are united against problems

Identified Quality of Healthy Family	S for a Strength Score	C for a Challenge Score
Appreciation	____	____
Spending Time Together	____	____
Good Communication Patterns	____	____
Commitments to Family	____	____
High Degree of Religious Orientation	____	____
Deals with Crisis in a Positive Way	____	____

funtastic family nights

It Takes More than Love

Bible Reading

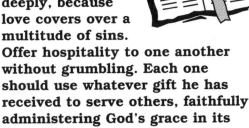

Above all, love each other deeply, because love covers over a multitude of sins. Offer hospitality to one another without grumbling. Each one should use whatever gift he has received to serve others, faithfully administering God's grace in its various forms. *(1 Peter 4:8–10)*

Family Time

Set aside some time to act out an important ritual of affirmation and love. One person starts and says, "How do I love you? Let me count the ways. I love _____ because of _____."

Go around the family circle, then begin again for each family member.

Prayer Time

Light a candle, turn off the lights, gather around the candle, hold hands, and pray the Lord's Prayer.

Reflection

It is clear to everyone, especially parents, that being able to hear is not the same as being able to listen. Children don't often listen to the instructions of parents. It is also true that parents often do not listen to the thoughts and feelings behind the words of their children.

Carl Rogers, a noted psychologist, said that to enjoy hearing someone is to "hear deeply." By this, he means hearing more than words. Hearing deeply includes hearing the thoughts and feelings of the person speaking. He reflects a style of listening that has been called "active" listening.

When we actively listen to one another, we are communicating our own sense of self-worth and how much we value the relationship. Listening requires greater skill and wisdom than speaking. Active listening requires intentional, singular focus on the speaker. With all the effort required to listen effectively, it's no wonder that listening is the language of love.

Think about the people in your life who have listened to you with focused attention. Can you remember how it made you feel about yourself and them? It is not a coincidence that our heavenly Father listens to us quietly, patiently, and knowingly, then acts in our behalf with grace and power.

16 Let There Be Peace

Key Concept

Our love for Jesus enables us to love one another. The family is a visual witness to the peace that Christ has brought into the world. Peace in the community begins with harmonious families.

Bible Passage

Romans 15:5–7

Objective

Participants will discover that keeping peace in the family is a way of glorifying Jesus, who is the Prince of Peace. They will discuss difficult issues of family rules and recognize that rules can be an extension of love and nurturing. They will imagine ways to act in peace with one another.

Materials Checklist

☐ Index cards

☐ Butcher paper or newsprint

☐ Name tags and markers

☐ Copies of the Family Event Handout (one for each participant)

☐ Copies of the Take-home Page (one for each participating family)

As Participants Arrive—Mural of Peace

Cover a wall of your meeting room with butcher paper or newsprint (as large as 4 feet tall and 20 feet long). Draw a large manger in the center of the mural with the title "Prince of Peace" arched over the manger. As people arrive, ask them to prepare a name tag. Then invite them to draw themselves into the mural, demonstrating acts of peace. They can use words, symbols, or drawings, but they must somehow include themselves in the mural.

Opening Prayer

Gather everyone and pray the prayer of St. Francis:

Lord, make me an instrument of Your peace.
Where there is hatred, let me sow love;
where there is injury, pardon;
where there is doubt, faith;
where there is darkness, light;
where there is sadness, joy.
Grant that I may not so much seek
to be consoled as to console;
to be understood as to understand;
to be loved as to love.
For it is in giving that we receive;
it is in pardoning that we are pardoned;
and it is in dying that we are born to
eternal life.

For Starters

Announce the theme with the following thoughts:

Tonight we are going to explore "the peace that passes all understanding." You will talk about some things that may not be peaceful topics, yet the goal is to imagine ways that Jesus could help us find harmony, even in matters of conflict.

Ask for volunteers to come up to the mural and explain what they have drawn. When everyone has had an opportunity to share, make the observation that peace is not a program for a church committee, but it is a gift of Christ to the world. It comes to life through individuals acting in ways that glorify the one who is the Prince of Peace. Our families can be witnesses to God's love and hope for a peaceful community.

Handout Facilitation Suggestions

Ask the groups to send one person to gather the necessary materials from the supply table at the appropriate time. Remind them that even if smaller children may not respond to the questions, they will grow from being a part of the family discussion.

Give a copy of the handout to each person at the tables. Instruct them to respond to the questions and activities. Keep groups aware of the time and encourage them to move on to each portion of the handout.

Closing

Sing "Let There Be Peace on Earth."

Pass out the Take-home Page as families leave.

Let There Be Peace

Focus (5 minutes)

Practice reading this passage together until your family sounds like one voice glorifying Jesus.

> **May the God who gives endurance and encouragement give you a spirit of unity among yourselves as you follow Christ Jesus, so that with one heart and mouth you may glorify the God and Father of our Lord Jesus Christ.**
>
> **Accept one another, then, just as Christ accepted you, in order to bring praise to God. (Romans 15:5–7)**

Activity—Peace for the Glory of God (20 minutes)

The following discussion brings up issues that usually bring disharmony to the home. The list includes a careful balance between rules that are designed to "control behavior" and rules that are designed to "bring peace and harmony" while teaching self-discipline and self-respect.

Fill in the following continuum and compare your differing scores. The lower the score, the more you see your family as based on helpful rules that encourage responsibility. A higher score indicates a tendency toward "controlled" behavior.

Give each person a chance to discuss his or her score without interruptions. Then after everyone has shared, respond to the following: How does our family harmony glorify Jesus?

Rules for Peaceful Family Life						Rules for Controlled Behavior
A few important rules	1	2	3	4	5	Lots and lots of rules
Let kids manage their time	1	2	3	4	5	Limit kids' time (TV, sleep, etc.)
Concern about drugs	1	2	3	4	5	Often search rooms for drugs
Let kids pick friends	1	2	3	4	5	Friends must be parents' type
Concern for grades	1	2	3	4	5	Ask about homework daily
Concern about safety	1	2	3	4	5	Overly anxious about safety
Let kids manage money	1	2	3	4	5	Control how kids spend money

Total _____

Closing (5 minutes)

Using the index cards, write a Care Card to each person in your family. The Care Card could be anything you promise to do to show you care.

Share the cards with each other. End your time together with a prayer that Christ would bring peace and joy into your home.

Mom,
I will give you two hugs every day for one week.
Love, Kevin

funtastic family nights

Let There Be Peace

Bible Reading

May the God who gives endurance and encouragement give you a spirit of unity among yourselves as you follow Christ Jesus, so that with one heart and mouth you may glorify the God and Father of our Lord Jesus Christ.

Accept one another, then, just as Christ accepted you, in order to bring praise to God. (Romans 15:5–7)

Reflection

Children are emotional barometers. They tend to reflect the emotional well-being of the significant adults in their life. As parents, when you observe a conflict or crisis in the lives of your children, you need to first look to your own life for factors that may be creating or adding to that conflict and anxiety.

Parents lead the way in creating an atmosphere of peace and harmony in the home. Parents need to be the first to forgive, the first to hug, the first to smile, the first to tell the truth, the first to celebrate, the first to worship. Husbands and wives can model peace and harmony in their relationship, even if they are divorced. This kind of "adult" behavior is possible when we reflect upon our relationship with Jesus Christ. Jesus loved us first! It is because of our love, honor, and respect for Him that we love, honor, and respect our children.

Family Time—Planning a Day of Peace and Joy

Plan a family day that includes activities that the whole family can do together. Avoid things that are passive entertainment, such as amusement parks or movies. Give everyone a chance to decide on an activity that will happen on your Day of Peace and Joy. Include the following decisions:

- What day can we set aside for everyone to participate?
- How many hours will we have?
- How much are you willing to spend? (Keep this amount low to inspire creativity.)
- What are each of your activity choices?
- How can we schedule all our choices into a plan for the day?
- How can we all work together to get the needed materials and supplies?

Possible ideas might include a hike, picnic, board games, music, car trip, bake together, build something, gift exchange, or jigsaw puzzle.

Others might add to an activity or adapt it but only with the permission of the one who suggested the activity. Everyone agrees to participate in the activity with equal time scheduled for everyone.

Prayer Time

Close with the prayer of St. Francis:

Lord, make me an instrument of Your peace.
    Where there is hatred, let me sow love;
    where there is injury, pardon;
    where there is doubt, faith;
    where there is darkness, light;
    where there is sadness, joy.
Grant that I may not so much seek
    to be consoled as to console;
    to be understood as to understand;
    to be loved as to love.
For it is in giving that we receive;
    it is in pardoning that we are pardoned; and
    it is in dying that we are born to eternal life.

funtastic family nights

17
When You Sing, You Pray Twice

Key Concept

Music is a wonderful way to worship and bring the family together. There are many ways to use music in the home.

Bible Passage

Psalm 98

Objective

Participants will explore their gift for music making and music appreciation. They will practice using music as a way to praise God and a way to bring a spirit of unity to the family.

If this event is done during the Advent or Christmas season, you can substitute songs and carols of the season for the music.

Materials Checklist

☐ Tape or CD player

☐ Newsprint or butcher paper (a sheet for each family)

☐ Construction paper

☐ Markers

☐ Yarn

☐ Copies of the Family Event Handout (one for each participant)

☐ Copies of the Take-home Page (one for each participating family)

As Participants Arrive

Make large name cards with a string for wearing around the neck. Place 8½″ × 11″ construction paper and markers on the table and invite all to write their names on one of the name tags and the title of their favorite song.

For Starters

Demonstrate a few bars on your air guitar (pretend strumming a guitar) while you announce that the evening will celebrate the gift of music in our homes.

Invite participants to mill about for a few minutes looking at one another's name tags. Ask them to find anyone with the same favorite song.

Ask everyone to think of their favorite Christmas carol. Tell them to start singing the song and find others who are singing "their" song. When they find the others, they should stand in a circle and keep singing the first stanza over and over. When everyone has found their song mates (combine the individuals who did not find a group into a group of their own), tell them to take turns completing the following sentence: If I were a musical instrument, I would be …

Handout Facilitation Suggestions

Ask the groups to send one person to gather the necessary materials from the supply table at the appropriate time. Remind them that even if smaller children may not respond to the questions, they will grow from being a part of the family discussion.

Give a copy of the handout to each person at the tables. Instruct them to respond to the questions and activities. Keep groups aware of the time and encourage them to move on to each portion of the handout.

Some families may not be comfortable with music in their family circle. It is important not to make them uncomfortable with the song writing exercise. Encourage them to go as far with the activity as possible but to adapt it so they can participate in a way that works for them.

Closing

Invite families to share their songs. Hold up the words for all to sing. Sing as many songs as the groups are willing to share or as time allows.

Read the following psalm as a closing prayer.

Sing to the LORD a new song,
*   for He has done marvelous things;*
His right hand and His holy arm
*   have worked salvation for Him.*
The LORD has made His salvation known
*   and revealed His righteousness to the*
*   nations.*
He has remembered His love
*   and His faithfulness to the house of Israel;*
all the ends of the earth have seen
*   the salvation of our God.*
Shout for joy to the LORD, all the earth,
*   burst into jubilant song with music;*
make music to the LORD with the harp,
*   with the harp and the sound of singing,*
with trumpets and the blast of the ram's
*   horn—*
*   shout for joy before the LORD, the King.*
Let the sea resound, and everything in it,
*   the world, and all who live in it.*
Let the rivers clap their hands,
*   let the mountains sing together for joy;*
let them sing before the LORD,
*   for He comes to judge the earth.*
He will judge the world in righteousness
*   and the peoples with equity. (Psalm 98)*

Pass out the Take-home Page as families leave.

When You Sing, You Pray Twice

Activity (15 minutes)

Play "Name That Tune." One person thinks of a song and a hint about the song. They hum the first three notes of the song. The first person to the right tries to guess the song. If he or she cannot guess the song, the next person to the right tries. If no one in the family can guess the tune, add two more notes and go around the circle again. Keep adding notes until someone guesses the song. The person who guesses correctly thinks of a new song and the process is repeated.

Focus (5 minutes)

Ask someone to read the following "song" from the Bible.

*Sing to the LORD a new song,
  for He has done marvelous things;
His right hand and His holy arm
  have worked salvation for Him.
The LORD has made His salvation known
  and revealed His righteousness to the
    nations.
He has remembered His love
  and His faithfulness to the house of Israel;
all the ends of the earth have seen
  the salvation of our God.
Shout for joy to the LORD, all the earth,
  burst into jubilant song with music;
make music to the LORD with the harp,
  with the harp and the sound of singing,
with trumpets and the blast of the ram's
    horn—
  shout for joy before the LORD, the King.
Let the sea resound, and everything in it,
  the world, and all who live in it.
Let the rivers clap their hands,
  let the mountains sing together for joy;
let them sing before the LORD,
  for He comes to judge the earth.
He will judge the world in righteousness
  and the peoples with equity. (Psalm 98)*

Activity—God Has Shown His Love for Us (20 minutes)

Work together to write a song with the title "God Has Shown His Love for Us" to the melody of "Michael, Row the Boat Ashore."

Write the words on a large sheet of newsprint or butcher paper. Hold it up and sing it together.

When You Sing, You Pray Twice

Bible Reading

Come, let us sing for joy to the LORD;
let us shout aloud to the Rock of our
salvation.
Let us come before Him with thanksgiving
and extol Him with music and song.
For the Lord is the great God,
the great King above all gods.
In His hand are the depths of the earth,
and the mountain peaks belong to Him.
The sea is His, for He made it,
and His hands formed the dry land.
Come, let us bow down in worship,
let us kneel before the LORD our Maker.
(Psalm 95:1–6)

Reflection

Next to theology I give to music the highest place and honor. Music is the art of the prophets, the only art that can calm the agitations of the soul: it is one of the most magnificent and delightful presents God has given us. *Martin Luther*

Music is a wonderful gift to the family. Families can use music to praise God and grow closer together.

Family Time

Set aside some time to have a music appreciation evening. Each member should select one piece of music that the entire family will listen to. Having the words available would be helpful.

Everyone in turn announces their selection and tells why they like it.

Conclude with a recording of sacred music appropriate to the age of your children. If you do not have such a CD or audiocassette, you might make this a family project to choose some music.

funtastic family nights

The Power of Love

18

Key Concept

The ability to influence another person is often referred to as personal power. This power to influence is very important in the relationship between parents and children. The greatest power of all is the power of unconditional love, which engenders responding affection and a willingness to serve. Coercive power (the use of rewards and punishments) can be effective in the short-term. However, it has limited capacity to nurture and develop abiding values.

Bible Passage

Luke 22:24–27

Objective

This family event is designed to help participants consider the various types of power family members use to influence one another. Participants will discover that service is God's idea of influential authority. Family members will consider who has the power in their family and why.

Materials Checklist

☐ Newsprint

☐ Markers

☐ 8½″ × 11″ paper (one for each participant)

☐ Hole punch

☐ String

☐ Copies of the Family Event Handout (one for each participant)

☐ Copies of the Take-home Page (one for each participating family)

As Participants Arrive

Ask each person to make a name necklace. Use markers and a 8½″ × 11″ sheet of paper with holes punched in the corners. Hang the finished page around the neck with string.

Participants write their names in the middle and one thing they do best in each corner of the paper.

Opening Prayer

Dear heavenly Father, You have revealed Your love for us in the person of Jesus of Nazareth. Help us to be people who show love— love for You, love for ourselves, and love for one another. Amen.

For Starters

Ask everyone to stand in the center of the room. Tell the group that they have three minutes to get in a line from oldest to youngest. Infants in arms will be accounted for after everyone is in place. Encourage everyone to learn the name of the people standing next to them.

Second, participants are to line up from tallest to shortest. Take notice of the changes in the line. Ask the group to bend the line into a circle. While they are in the large circle, introduce the theme with the following statement:

This event is all about power in the family. I have asked you to line up from the oldest to the youngest and the tallest to the shortest. We are able to do that quite easily. However, if I were to ask you to line up from the most powerful to the least powerful, it would be difficult to do. Jesus knew that we often want to know who is the best or the greatest, so He taught this lesson. (Go to the smallest child and stand next to him or her.) Jesus said whoever wants to be greatest in the kingdom of heaven should become as this child. He said if you want to be powerful, you need to be a servant.

Handout Facilitation Suggestions

Ask the groups to send one person to gather the necessary materials from the supply table at the appropriate time. Remind them that even if smaller children may not respond to the questions, they will grow from being a part of the family discussion.

Give a copy of the handout to each person at the tables. Instruct them to respond to the questions and activities. Keep groups aware of the time and encourage them to move on to each portion of the handout.

Closing

Dear friends and families in Christ, go to your homes with this blessing from St. Paul, "Now to Him who is able to do immeasurably more than all we ask or imagine, according to His power that is at work within us, to Him be glory in the church and in Christ Jesus throughout all generations, for ever and ever! Amen." (Ephesians 3:20–21)

Pass out the Take-home Page as families leave.

The Power of Love

Focus (10 minutes)

Think of each person in your family and list them in order, beginning with the most powerful to the least powerful. Also, think of reasons why you have ranked them in that way. Think of reasons other than age.

Ask someone to read the following passage aloud:

> **Also a dispute arose among them as to which of them was considered to be greatest. Jesus said to them, "The kings of the Gentiles lord it over them; and those who exercise authority over them call themselves Benefactors. But you are not to be like that. Instead, the greatest among you should be like the youngest, and the one who rules like the one who serves. For who is greater, the one who is at the table or the one who serves? Is it not the one who is at the table? But I am among you as one who serves."** *(Luke 22:24–27)*

According to this passage, who are the greatest ones in your family?

Closing (10 minutes)

Draw a large heart over the entire newsprint page and read the following aloud:

> **We might say the reason we do these acts of service is because of the importance to our family's well-being. Yet the real reason we do them is because we love one another. It is the love we have for each other that motivates us to serve. Love is the greatest. Love is powerful.**

Use the newsprint as a formula for your prayer time. Insert the information from the newsprint into the following sentence. Repeat the sentence for each item listed. You could ask one person to read all the sentences or each person can read one, going around the family until all are read.

> **Dear Jesus, we are thankful for the service of *(name of service)*. It helps our family because *(cite the importance of the service)*, and it is a sign of our love. Amen.**

Activity—Service Brainstorm (15 minutes)

Take newsprint and markers. Divide the newsprint into two columns. In the first column list all the things that are done in your family to serve the family. In the second column note why that action is important to the family. Don't list who does the action, simply list every service you can possibly think of. Each person should share one idea and why it is important. Then go around the family circle over and over until you have filled the newsprint.

Service	Importance
cook meals	healthy growth
cleans rooms	saves time
does laundry	clothes to wear

The Power of Love

Bible Reading

Also a dispute arose among them as to which of them was considered to be greatest. Jesus said to them, "The kings of the Gentiles lord it over them; and those who exercise authority over them call themselves Benefactors. But you are not to be like that. Instead, the greatest among you should be like the youngest, and the one who rules like the one who serves. For who is greater, the one who is at the table or the one who serves? Is it not the one who is at the table? But I am among you as one who serves." *(Luke 22:24–27)*

Family Time

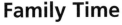

Set aside a time to talk about power in your family. Ask this question of each person in your family: How do you get each of the others in our family to do things for you? Spend some time thinking about each person. Take turns sharing your thoughts. Give everyone a chance to share before you begin any discussion. Then answer the following questions:

• What are the signs of unconditional love in your family?

• How can you work together and seek God's love to build up the "love power" in your family?

Prayer Time

Write the name of each person in your family and what you appreciate about them. Now take turns sharing what you have written. Close with a prayer with each person saying what they appreciate about Jesus.

Take-home PAGE

The Power of Love

Reflection—Who's Got the Power?

Everyone in the family has power or the ability to influence others in some way. Love is a powerful influence, yet sometimes what looks like an act of love and kindness may be manipulative. Think about the people in your family and consider the following types of influencing power.

Reward Power. This is based on someone's ability (or the perception that they have the ability) to give rewards such as money, recognition, or other favors. A reward may be an increase in something positive or a decrease in something negative. The parent may say, "When you clean your room, you may watch television." The child may say, "You are a great mom!" or "You are mean!"

Coercive Power. This power is also based on an individual's ability to control something that another person needs. This power often appears as promises or threats. To have this power you have to create fear that someone will be punished by withholding what is desired (resources, rewards, cooperation) or delivering what is not desired. The exercise of this type of power is likely to result in resistance. When children are young, you can give them a treat or send them to their room. When they get older and more powerful, you may have to give them a car or take away the car.

Expert Power. This power is based on special knowledge, skill, or expertise. Parents possess vast and powerful resources of expert power for the good of their children— "Daddy, how does this work?" or "I would like to start my own savings account, what do I do?" When the child is genuinely interested, there is great opportunity to teach. When instruction comes from the parent's need to teach, however, the child is less receptive. The willingness to accept information is the primary factor in how effective the influence will be. The actual content of the information imparted is secondary.

Legitimate Power. This is based on the individual's position or right to exercise power. The position of parent is a legitimate position of authority. The Bible is clear about the role of parent in the family. Note, however, that the child who is being influenced also must understand that the position of parent is legitimate. During the teenage years this power is often challenged, especially if the parent uses a combination of legitimate power and coercive power.

Love Power. When it comes to influencing others, our best and most powerful choice is to change our own behavior. We are not able to change others, only influence them. If we love and accept them as people who are loved, chosen, and redeemed by God, we will have a powerful influence on how they behave. The power shifts from "what I have" to "what the relationship has."

funtastic family nights

19
Celebrating God in Nature

This event focuses on one of the best places for family faith talk. It is not around a table; it is in God's natural world. Consider the following suggestions for creating opportunities for faith talk.

Think about the message of this psalm.

The heavens declare the glory of God;
    the skies proclaim the work of His hand.
Day after day they pour forth speech;
    night after night they display knowledge.
There is no speech or language
    where their voice is not heard.
Their voice goes out into all the earth,
    their words to the ends of the world.
In the heavens He has pitched a tent for the sun,
    which is like a bridegroom coming forth from
        his pavilion,
    like a champion rejoicing to run his course.
It rises at one end of the heavens
    and makes its circuit to the other;
    nothing is hidden from its heat.
The law of the LORD is perfect,
    reviving the soul.
The statutes of the LORD are trustworthy,
    making wise the simple.
The precepts of the LORD are right,
    giving joy to the heart.
The commands of the LORD are radiant,
    giving light to the eyes.
The fear of the LORD is pure,
    enduring forever.
The ordinances of the LORD are sure
    and altogether righteous.
They are more precious than gold,
    than much pure gold;
they are sweeter than honey,
    than honey form the comb.
By them is Your servant warned;
    in keeping them there is great reward.
Who can discern his errors?
    Forgive my hidden faults.
Keep Your servant also from willful sins;
    may they not rule over me.
Then will I be blameless,
    innocent of great transgression.
May the words of my mouth and the meditation
        of my heart
    be pleasing in Your sight,
    O LORD, my Rock and my Redeemer.
(Psalm 19)

Suggestions for Family Nature Talks

Family Picnic

Everyone plans the picnic together and takes part in the work to get ready. While on the picnic, talk about your favorite part of the outdoors.

Head for the Nearest Park

Next time you go for fast-food, plan to eat it in the park. While you are there, play a game of freeze tag.

Go Camping in Your Backyard

Borrow a tent (if you don't have one) and spend the evening together in the backyard. Candles and flashlights can bring the family together and also bring out the conversations. Parents might decide to spend the entire evening telling stories about their childhood.

Backyard Planetarium

Get a book on the stars and constellations from the library. Read it yourself in preparation for this event, or read it together. Check when known meteor showers will occur. Watch the weather reports to select a clear night sky. When it begins to get dark, lay out a large blanket in your backyard. Turn off and block out as many lights as possible. Then lie on your backs, looking up to the heavens. Watch for shooting stars and satellites.

Family Servants

Form a rake brigade. With rakes and trash bags, your family would be a welcome sight for any neighbor who is a senior citizen or disabled. Raking is an activity that has roles for everyone: raking, bagging, hauling, and jumping in the piles.

Sunrise, Sunset

Find any good-sized body of water. Plan to be there one half hour before the sun comes up or before the sun sets.

Watch the Sky

On a day when the clouds are fluffy and white, lay a blanket on the grass and lie back to watch the pictures go by. When someone spots an animal, a person, or a symbol in the clouds, he or she describes it for the others. While watching the clouds, keep an eye out for God's handiwork.

What Is Watching You?

Give a flashlight to everyone in your family. Go to a woods or a park at night and shine for eyes. You will be amazed at how many eyes will look back. The eyes of frogs and toads, spiders, birds, and raccoons will all reflect as colored points of light.

Family Fishing Trip

Take everyone on your next trip to the fishing hole. The more experienced fisherpersons should remember to keep a focus on family togetherness, not the size and amount of fish.

Plant Something

As a family, go to the nursery and have each child pick out a plant that is within your budget. When you get home, everyone works to plant their choice in a choice spot.

Snow Picnic

Take a walk in the winter woods to a place for a picnic. The suggested menu includes chili and hot chocolate with marshmallows.

The Snow Family

Make a snowman for everyone in your family. Build the "snow family" in the front yard and send a greeting to the neighborhood. Take a picture for your photo album.

Family Nature Talk

Take your family to a favorite spot in nature. That may be at the ocean, in the woods, by a mountain, next to a stream, or perhaps your backyard provides a good view of God's handiwork.

Find a comfortable spot where you can see and hear one another. Choose a location where you will not be interrupted by others.

Read the questions aloud and give everyone in your family a chance to respond. It is okay to pass.

1. What do you like about this spot?

2. What is mysterious or interesting to you?

3. What are your earliest memories about being out in nature?

Ask someone to read the psalm aloud. Think about how the writer refers to nature to proclaim God's glory.

> O LORD, our Lord,
>   how majestic is Your name
>   in all the earth!
> You have set Your glory
>   above the heavens.
> From the lips of children and infants
>   You have ordained praise
> because of Your enemies,
>   to silence the enemy and the avenger.
> When I consider Your heavens,
>   the work of Your fingers,
> the moon and the stars,
>   which You have set in place,
> what is man that You are mindful of him,
>   the son of man that You care for him?
> You made him a little lower than the
>   heavenly beings
>   and crowned him with glory and honor.
> You made him ruler over the works of
>   Your hands;
>   You put everything under his feet:
> all flocks and herds,
>   and the beasts of the field,
> the birds of the air,
>   and the fish of the sea,
>   all that swim the paths of the seas.
> O LORD, our Lord,
>   how majestic is Your name in all the earth!
>   (Psalm 8)

4. How important are you to God according to this psalm? What does it mean that "You are mindful of him" right now?

5. What does *ruler* mean in this passage? What are you doing to everything under your feet?

Give everyone time to think of a prayer that completes this sentence:

Lord, You have blessed me in my family by ...

Close by having everyone pray their prayers.